Praise for *Speak Up*

'Your career, organisation and society at large will be well served if you take time to reflect and act upon this book's core messages.'

Andrew Brammer, CIO, Allen & Overy LLP

'THE how-to guide to navigating the power and politics of conversations at work.'

Des Dearlove and Stuart Crainer, Thinkers50

'Speaking truth to power has never been more critical than it feels today, but finding our voice and helping others find theirs requires awareness, compassion and skill. Megan and John's research into the complexities of speaking our truth has resulted in one of the best "how-to" guides I have read in a long time.'

Marina Bolton, HR Director, Organisation Development, Design and Learning, UK Civil Service

'Creating the right conditions for individuals to speak up is a critical organisational capability. This book will trigger reflections and provide tools to do so.'

Céline Shakouri-Dias, Head, Talent and Organisational Development, North Atlantic Treaty Organization (NATO)

'The world of sport is all about the character of people in a highly pressured environment. The quality of conversations is a critical component of character and this book gives you a clear structure on how to say what matters when it really matters - before the event not later when the pressure is off and it is too late to make a difference to the result.'

John Neal, Head of Coach Development, English Cricket Board

'Megan and John's research is a timely and crucial guide for leaders in how they can influence organisational culture towards openness and respect.'

John Shropshire, Chairman, G's Fresh

'With such rapid change, leaders need to make decisions quickly, thoughtfully and ethically – they can't do this unless they speak up well and enable others to do the same. This book tells you how.'

Mark Esposito, Professor of Business and Economics, Hult International Business School; Member of the Teaching Faculty at Harvard University

'Oh, what a tangled web we weave, observed Sir Walter Scott. Megan Reitz and John Higgins give us a fascinating insight into the tangled web of power, silence and the art of speaking up. If you want to have more of a voice or help others to have one, read this book. It is not to be missed.'

Richard Badham, Professor of Management, Macquarie Business School and Graduate School of Management. Author of Ironies of Organizational Change (Edward Elgar, 2020) and co-author of Power, Politics and Organizational Change (Sage, Third Edition 2020)

'Full of valuable insights and concrete actions, *Speak Up* is a compelling read for all those wishing to create a more open, thriving and productive environment within their organisation.'

Derek Hammond, Managing Director, Head of Culture and Conduct UK, Societe Generale

'*Speak Up* is full of important lessons about the impact we have on people around us. It is not just about speaking up, but understanding why others may not in your presence - a crucial lesson if you want to lead effectively.'

Mark Davies, Chairman British Rowing

'Open dialogue is critical to personal and organisational performance. Megan's 'Speak Up' work with us in Vestey has shone a light on how we communicate and given us the means to influence our conversational habits for the better.'

George Vestey, CEO Vestey Holdings

'*Speak Up* is a powerful book on an important topic. Authors Megan Reitz and John Higgins offer a compassionate perspective on speaking up at work as they take us readers through the subtle elements that contribute to our holding back valuable ideas and observations. Their TRUTH framework – which is as practical as it is rigorous – identifies essential elements to help individuals find their voice.'

Amy Edmondson, Professor, Harvard Business School, author, The Fearless Organization *(Wiley, 2019)*

'Stop telling people to speak up; instead, set up the social spaces so a person is actually heard. Reitz and Higgins show us how to do more than try harder to overcome ideas being silenced.'

Nilofer Merchant, author, Power of Onlyness

'Finding our voice and helping others find theirs requires awareness, compassion and skill. This book provides a vital how-to guide to developing these and opening dialogue in our workplace.'

Michael Chaskalson, bestselling author, Mindfulness in 8 Weeks *and* Mind Time; *Thinkers50 Radar*

'After thirty years across military, management consulting, banking and private equity organisations, I find myself fascinated by the fact that speaking up well is a sign of an outperformance culture. This is so rarely explicit and understood. Participation in this study at the early stages and now benefiting from this book have been a positive and powerful experience for my role in leadership in organisations.'

Ruwan Weerasekera, formerly COO Trading & Sales, UBS Investment Bank and Senior Independent Director, ICBC Standard Bank

'John Higgins taught me how to speak truth to power. A cathartic experience that allowed me to be heard and remain true to myself. His brilliant new book, co-authored with Megan Reitz, *Speak Up* is an indispensable, practical guide for everyone who wants to increase their personal impact in any work situation.'

Diana Choyleva, Chief Economist, Enodo Economics;
author, The Bill in the China Shop

SPEAK UP

Pearson

At Pearson, we believe in learning – all kinds of learning for all kinds of people. Whether it's at home, in the classroom or in the workplace, learning is the key to improving our life chances.

That's why we're working with leading authors to bring you the latest thinking and best practices, so you can get better at the things that are important to you. You can learn on the page or on the move, and with content that's always crafted to help you understand quickly and apply what you've learned.

If you want to upgrade your personal skills or accelerate your career, become a more effective leader or more powerful communicator, discover new opportunities or simply find more inspiration, we can help you make progress in your work and life.

Every day our work helps learning flourish, and wherever learning flourishes, so do people.

To learn more, please visit us at **www.pearson.com/uk**

The Financial Times

With a worldwide network of highly respected journalists, *The Financial Times* provides global business news, insightful opinion and expert analysis of business, finance and politics. With over 500 journalists reporting from 50 countries worldwide, our in-depth coverage of international news is objectively reported and analysed from an independent, global perspective.

To find out more, visit **www.ft.com**

Megan Reitz
John Higgins

SPEAK UP

SAY WHAT NEEDS TO BE SAID AND HEAR WHAT NEEDS TO BE HEARD

Pearson

Harlow, England • London • New York • Boston • San Francisco • Toronto • Sydney
Dubai • Singapore • Hong Kong • Tokyo • Seoul • Taipei • New Delhi
Cape Town • São Paulo • Mexico City • Madrid • Amsterdam • Munich • Paris • Milan

PEARSON EDUCATION LIMITED
KAO Two
KAO Park
Harlow
CM17 9SR
United Kingdom
Tel: +44 (0)1279 623623
Web: www.pearson.com/uk

First edition published 2019 (print and electronic)
© Pearson Education Limited 2019 (print and electronic)

ISBN: 978-1-292-26301-4 (print)
      978-1-292-26302-1 (PDF)
      978-1-292-26303-8 (ePub)

British Library Cataloguing-in-Publication Data
A catalogue record for the print edition is available from the British Library

Library of Congress Cataloging-in-Publication Data
A catalog record for the print edition is available from the Library of Congress

10 9 8 7 6 5 4 3 2 1
23 22 21 20 19

Cover design by Two Associates

Print edition typeset in 9.5/13, Helvetica Neue LT W1G by SPi Global
Printed by Ashford Colour Press Ltd, Gosport

NOTE THAT ANY PAGE CROSS REFERENCES REFER TO THE PRINT EDITION

To

Steve, Mia & Charlotte

And

Rosie, Livia & Isobel

CONTENTS

ABOUT THE AUTHORS

Megan Reitz is Professor of Leadership and Dialogue at Ashridge Executive Education, Hult International Business School, where she speaks, researches, consults and supervises on the intersection of leadership, change, dialogue and mindfulness. She is on the Thinkers50 radar of global business thinkers and is ranked in *HR Magazine's* Most Influential Thinker listing. She has presented her research to audiences throughout the world and is the author of *Dialogue in Organisations* and *Mind Time.* Her passion and curiosity centres around the quality of how we meet, see, hear, speak, learn with and care for one another in organisational systems. She is mother to two wonderful daughters who test her regularly and rigorously on her powers of mindfulness and dialogue.

John Higgins approaches life as a continuous research project, integrating the personal and professional, and finding ways to bring the hidden habits of work into the light of day. He is Research Director at The Right Conversation, where he's working to develop a 'Speak-up index' (a measure of organisational transparency), and Research Fellow at Gameshift. He has written widely on organisational change as part of his role on the Ashridge Doctorate and Masters in Organisational Change and his work draws heavily on insights from his long-standing engagement with the psychoanalytic process.

ACKNOWLEDGEMENTS

We would like to thank everyone who has been part of the research that underpins this book. Unsurprisingly many cannot be identified because of commercial and organizational sensitivity and because public identification would change what they felt able to say. However, you know who you are and we hope we have done your voices justice in this book.

Those who can be named include the unstinting Ashridge research team at Hult International Business School, in particular Viktor Nilsson, Emma Day and Grace Brown, who have supported our work with such enthusiasm and discipline and to Erika Lucas for her tireless assistance in publicising and communicating our findings and ideas. Our thanks also to the team at FT Pearson, especially Eloise Cook, our editor, for her invaluable guidance.

Lastly a big thank you to Julian Burton at Delta7, who spent many hours with us teasing out how to summarise our findings in terms of artistic illustration – and helped us know our work through a fresh lens.

PUBLISHER'S ACKNOWLEDGEMENTS

Text credits:

xxi **Lew Platt:** Lew Platt, CEO of one time technology colossus Hewlett Packard **xxii Bernd Osterloh:** Bernd Osterloh, The chief of the VW works council, https://www.reuters.com/article/us-volkswagen-emissions-culture-idUSKCN0S40MT20151010 **xxiv BigCo. SmallCo.:** Jeff', Head of Merger Integration in the Advertising and Social Media world, 'SmallCo-BigCo' **4 Simon:** Simon **26 Maya Angelou, The poet, writer and civil rights activist:** Maya Angelou **27 Sheryl Sandberg:** Sheryl Sandberg, COO of Facebook **27 Professor Laura Empson:** Professor Laura Empson **27 Philosopher Bertrand Russell:** Philosopher Bertrand Russell **27 Robert W. Fuller:** Robert Fuller, Rankism **31 Michael Jordan:** Michael Jordan, the basketball megastar **43 Simon:** Simon **44 Drew Feustel:** Drew Feustel **44 Mike Massimino:** Mike Massimino is a former NASA astronaut **46 Professor Luis Garicano:** Professor Luis Garicano **52 Samuel Goldwyn:** Samuel Goldwyn, the American Film producer **68 Alan Mulally:** Alan Mulally, former President of Ford Motor Company **74 Julian Burton:** Julian Burton **88 Mahzarin Banaji:** Harvard University researcher Mahzarin Banaji **88 Random House:** Banaji and Greenwald, Blind Spot **89 Ben Fuchs:** Ben Fuchs **95 Thabo Makgoba:** Archbishop Thabo Makgoba from South Africa **96 Random House:** Banaji and Greenwald, Blind Spot **110 John:** ex-CEO, John **126 Pegasus Books:** Groth and Nitzberg, Solomon's Code. **127 Bloomsbury Publishing:** Arthur Weasley in the Harry Potter Book **137 Mark Zukerberg:** 2004, Mark Zukerberg, Facebook

All other cartoon images © Julian Burton

INTRODUCTION

Today, like every other day, you will choose when to speak up and when to stay silent. You will select whose opinion to listen to and whose to disregard.

Your choices have and will turn into habits which determine whether you get promoted or side-lined. Whether you steer clear of trouble or land right in it. Whether you feel proud of yourself or ashamed for what you have or have not said. Whether you flourish and feel motivated or end up dissatisfied and resentful.

Seemingly mundane acts of speaking and listening become habitual and profoundly influence how you see yourself and how others see you. They have defining consequences for you and those around you.

In this book you will learn how your perceptions of relative power, status and authority drive what you and your colleagues say and who you listen to. Although these perceptions are often unconscious, you need to be skilful at acknowledging, observing and influencing them in order to make better choices.

Reading this book will help you to do the following:

- Realise what stops you speaking up and being heard at work.
- Learn how to speak up with confidence and be heard effectively.
- Understand how to increase your personal impact by making the agenda and not just following it.
- Spot how you silence others and learn how to make it easy for people to speak openly to you.
- Create a working environment that is more innovative, honest, productive and fulfilling.

Wherever you sit in the organisational hierarchy, you will find out what you can do to make speaking up feel safe and useful.

Through our research, based on hundreds of interviews and survey responses, ethnographic studies and action research inquiries, we have developed a practical TRUTH framework. You'll discover in this book how it can change conversations, relationships and performance.

It sets out five questions which are vital to answer if you want to speak up and listen up more effectively:

1. How much do you **T**RUST the value of your opinion and the opinions of others?
2. What are the **R**ISKS involved when you or others speak up?
3. Do you **U**NDERSTAND the politics of who says what to who and why?
4. Are you aware of the **T**ITLES and labels we attach to one another – and how they shape what gets said and heard?
5. Do you know **H**OW to choose the right words at the right time in the right place and how, skilfully, to help others to speak up through what you say and do?

TIME TO LOOK IN THE MIRROR

Our research uncovered a critical blind spot in our capacity to improve conversations at work. Answering these questions might reveal it to you:

- Do you ever find yourself thinking: '*They* should speak up more'?
- Do you ever find yourself thinking: '*They* are scary – *they* should be more approachable'?

If you do, then you are far from alone. Our blind spot is that we tend to think that it is *other people* that need to change. While this may be the case, as we wait impatiently for them to do something differently, we can forget to look in the mirror and take responsibility for changing *our own* conversations.

All too often senior executives tell us that the problem lies with the rest of the organisation failing to have the courage to speak up.

'*They* just wait to be told what to do! *They* need to step up!'

'*They* need to start challenging things and coming up with ideas!'

So we go and talk with '*them*' – usually the middle management – who earnestly tell us that there is no way they can speak up as it would be career suicide or simply a waste of time.

'Did you hear what happened to the last person who challenged *them*? They disappeared!'

'*They* don't really care – *they*'ve already made up their minds.'

The point is this – speaking up is *relational*. It happens in-between someone being willing to say something and someone being willing and able to listen.

We know from all of the different strands of our research that we tend to think it's the other person's fault. The reason we don't speak up is because *that* person doesn't listen. The reason we don't listen up is because *that* person takes too long to get to the point or we assume *that* person just doesn't understand.

We know that we tend to value our own opinion around a third more than the opinion of others (in some groups we looked at, this went as high as three times).

We know that we tend to believe we are approachable and therefore assume others wouldn't hide things from us.

We know that if each one of us alters how we speak and listen, even marginally, whole cultures can change.

As individuals, teams, organisations and societies, we need to stop the blame game, look in the mirror and face up to not only how we silence ourselves, but also how we silence others.

THE SOUND (AND COST) OF SILENCE

Silence is the missing voice in a conversation. It is the sound of the something that should have been said but hasn't been. It happens all the time.

Have you ever encountered a situation you know to be wrong but not said anything? Have you ever had an idea about how something could be improved but kept it to yourself? Ever come to the realisation that someone at work or at home hasn't told you something because they were too scared to, didn't want to embarrass you, thought there was no point, or believed it wasn't their place to tell you?

The silence of missing voices costs careers, relationships and lives. It means new ideas never see the light of day and obvious problems don't get sorted out. It can and regularly does bring global organisations to their knees.

Silence leads to the drama of a CEO being fired, the scandalous fraud splashed across the front pages and the public outcry when what seems to be too good to be true turns out to be just that. But these dramatic moments don't come out of nowhere; they build up, often imperceptibly, over time as we silence ourselves and others, one conversation at a time.

We absorb the rules for our social group: what we should say and what we shouldn't; whose opinion counts and whose doesn't. Undiscussables, the 'elephants in the room', develop and are kept alive through our ordinary habits of going along with how things are done round here. Work is not just about getting the job done, it's also about fitting in – being recognised as someone who belongs to the gang. This means that challenging the status quo, however wrong it is, is risky.

We interviewed Sophie, a new graduate. She had arrived enthusiastically in the quality control team and couldn't understand why a dangerous practice was being tolerated. She mentioned it to her boss but was given the brush-off. She said nothing more. She saw herself as the junior newbie and didn't want to make a fuss – it took her a while to land the job and she wanted to keep it. Six months in, she accepted it as how things are done. But then an accident happened that changed a colleague's life forever and Sophie now feels crushed and responsible. A preventable accident emerging from silence.

Put yourself in the shoes of Toni, a successful sales director we interviewed. Frighteningly propositioned by one of her company's most influential customers, she eventually plucked up the courage to talk to her stressed head of sales. His impatient first question was: 'Maybe you were sending out the wrong signals?' Confused, she felt at fault, didn't argue when she was taken off the account and stayed silent about her experience. She has since heard that a female colleague was harassed by the same client. Patterns of silence and silencing meant this was allowed to go on.

In contrast, Stuart, a talented marketing manager had arrived bearing the scars of his previous workplace. He had been silenced by the risk-averse, controlling owners. It took about a year for him to find his voice. A patient boss, who trusted in his capabilities, proved to Stuart, day after day, that he would be listened to and that mistakes are acceptable and even encouraged if they are learnt from, in the pursuit of new ideas. This bore fruit as he developed an astoundingly innovative campaign which shot the organisation's product to a market leadership position.

How do *you* get your voice heard? How do you know if something is going on in *your* workplace right now that will be the next front-page scandal? And how do you embolden others to offer their ideas so you can respond to a world of ever-shifting expectations?

The answer is you can't and won't, unless you know how to speak up and help others to in our messy, political world filled with ordinary people, brimming with hope, vulnerability, insight and ambition.

The solution comes from the same place as the problem – we must *un*silence ourselves and help others to do the same, one conversation at a time. We must begin to make choices today that mean it is less risky for *everyone* to speak up.

ANTHONY

Consider the situation of Anthony, a well-meaning COO of an international design company, and his team.

'Let me tell you about speaking truth to power,' said Anthony when we met him. 'When I joined this place people would turn their heads away from me when we passed in the corridors. Now, I'm pleased to say, they always make eye contact and speak to me. Before they disrespected me. Now they respect me.'

A week later, we facilitated a workshop with Anthony's team. They shared insights and stories, spoke candidly about their realities as aspiring leaders in their company. Then Anthony walked into the room and immediately the conversation shifted. We sensed the tension, saw that opinions were suddenly more guarded and carefully phrased. The enthusiasm and ideas vanished and were replaced by measured, politically acceptable words. He was invited to speak and he earnestly told them what he deemed they wanted to hear. What leadership really was. How hard he'd had to work. What they needed to do to rise to the challenge.

After he had left we asked the group what they didn't say to him.

'People make eye contact and speak up because they're scared of him and what he can do to them – he is after all in charge of the restructure.' It had nothing to do with respect, fear was the key.

Ah! What a double bind. No one could tell Anthony they were scared of him – because they were scared of him. Looking back, it feels like a missed opportunity. A moment when both sides might have learnt together, collaborated, innovated and felt inspired. Prospects of seeing and hearing each other moved yet further away, lost in a familiar pattern of senior people asserting a truth and junior people staying silent about their reality.

On the one hand this interaction doesn't matter too much. Just another moment in a 'here today, gone tomorrow' workshop. One you might well recognise. On the other hand, it matters enormously, especially when this conversation is part of the cultural norm. Over time, it chips away at our ideas, motivation and development. It sustains a world of day-to-day fake-believe, of conversations conducted from behind facades where we disguise what we really think.

A tipping point might come when we decide we've had enough of sitting on our hands – we speak up and deal with the consequences. Or we might just continue and end up being cynical, suspicious or oblivious. However much lip service is paid to diversity, we might resign ourselves to fitting in. To succeed as a woman for instance, we might decide, in the words of a senior female executive we interviewed, that we 'have to speak up more like a man in the eyes of men'.

The missed opportunities are profound as we stifle our own and others' capacity to be at our best as human beings.

WHY ARE YOU READING THIS BOOK?

We assume that at some level you are interested in developing the way that you speak and listen to others. You may want to change your team or organisational culture for the better. You probably have in mind reasons why this would be a good thing, but we'd ask you to really pay attention right now to your *intention*.

If your intention is to change your habits – and we all have habits around what we speak up about, as well as who we listen to – it is vital to be clear on the case for change. Changing habits is often tough and if you don't have a compelling case, it is likely you will take the path of least resistance and stay with what you know. Most people's habits are, after all, tried and tested – and for the most part have served them well enough.

There is both a business and moral case for speaking up and listening up. Let's look at these in more detail.

THE BUSINESS CASE #1: SPEAKING UP TO THRIVE

It is likely that you are well aware of the 'industrial revolution 4.0', or the fourth industrial revolution. You will have heard such authoritative projections as 38% of jobs in the US could be replaced by AI in the next 15 years.[1] You will have listened to some who argue that this new wave of automation will be the making of us all, freeing us up to do the work we want to do and do best[2] . . . and you will have heard those who paint terrifying scenarios about a world of fake news, social dislocation and weaponised mis-information.[3]

Of course, we simply can't be certain what the future holds for work. We live in yet another age of upheaval and uncertainty and we are trying to figure out what model of good leadership will enable us to *thrive*. While 'heroic leadership'[4] seems to be alive and well in politics, for better or for worse, in the workplace it is falling out of favour. Due to our uncertain and possibly tumultuous future, approaches that distribute accountability across organisations are gaining in popularity. There's a drive to harness the agency and ideas of *all* employees and encourage new thinking, collaboration and adaptability. It's over 20 years since the CEO of one-time technology colossus Hewlett Packard observed: 'If only HP knew what HP knows we would be three times more productive.' We recognise the benefits of transparency and collaboration but we still haven't cracked how to make it work in practice.

Organisations currently lauded as the most innovative in the world, such as Google, Unilever and Netflix, advocate the value of speaking up and listening up. What other way is there to generate the ideas that keep them disruptive, creative and ahead of the curve? But advocating such a culture is the easy thing, living it is quite another. Shifting from the centralised paradigm to a distributed paradigm is tricky. It requires us to change the way we have conversations – from the managed world of top-down direction towards a more inclusive, multi-voiced model. This is often deeply counter-cultural.

Our research data points to a challenge for many senior leaders. Getting people to speak up is often less about the less powerful having a voice and more about the more powerful *really* wanting to listen to others throughout the organisation.

But leaders may well have to listen if their organisations, and by default, themselves, are to *thrive*.

THE BUSINESS CASE #2: SPEAKING UP TO SURVIVE

In September 2015, an upstanding corporate giant was shown to be hiding a critical flaw. Volkswagen, considered by many as invincible, stood accused of intentionally tampering with diesel engine emissions controls so that they activated during laboratory testing but not out on the roads. During real driving situations, cars were emitting up to 40 times more nitrogen oxide than was apparently the case in the laboratory, breaking any number of national and international laws and regulatory standards.

Over the days following the breaking story, the VW stock price fell by one third and Group CEO Martin Winterkorn resigned, although not before the many senior executives received their annual bonus payment in full. In May 2018, Winterkorn was criminally indicted in the US on charges of fraud and conspiracy.[5]

Inevitably, there were employees at VW who knew what was going on and decided not to speak up about malpractice or, if they did, their concerns were not listened to at the highest levels. A single employee eventually broke the scandal by talking to the regulators. Some reports suggested that organisational culture and leadership style led to the cover-up. 'We need, in future, a climate in which problems aren't hidden but can be openly communicated to superiors . . . [where] it's possible and permissible to argue with your superior about the best way to go,' said Osterloh, the chief of the VW works council.[6]

Today, newspaper headlines are littered with organisational and institutional scandals: financial misreporting in Japan; sexual predation throughout Hollywood and far beyond; military personnel going into battle with inadequate equipment; modern slavery being tacitly accepted practice in global supply chains; food products being contaminated with rogue substances as a matter of course; doping in sport that calls into question whether any sporting hero or team is going to be worthy of long-term admiration.

Throughout the years of our research, scandals were a weekly occurrence from around the world and in every sector. It became a cliché to read that people in such and such an organisation had 'failed to speak truth to power', with severely detrimental consequences for customers, investors and the wider world.

It is extremely difficult to ensure water-tight governance and accountability that might prevent wrongdoing. The failed British outsourcing giant Carillion had been given a clean bill of health from its auditors and had satisfactorily self-evaluated its board effectiveness (as the UK Corporate Governance Code requires), just before it fell into a heap of financial mismanagement and undeliverable contracts that had been many years in the making. Directors and non-executive directors sign personal liability statements – but for things they cannot possibly control. In the finance sector, credit control committees, dealing with sums almost beyond imagining, have to try to stay on top of an impossible brief. We were surprised, when interviewing them, that any of them had any hair left.

Realising governance is only part of the answer: many organisations are urgently seeking to create more transparency where challenging and speaking up about misconduct are an integral aspect of culture. It has become a matter of organisational *survival* and of personal career sustainability.

Would you know if there was something going on around you at work that could change everything, for you and your organisation, if it were to be found out?

THE BUSINESS CASE #3: SPEAKING UP TO STRIVE

The degree to which our opinion counts is, according to Gallup's famous research on employee engagement,[7] a critical factor in how motivated and engaged we are at work.

The problem is only three out of ten of us strongly agree that our opinion counts. According to Gallup, if that figure was more like six out of ten, organisations could realise a 27% reduction in staff turnover, a 40% reduction in safety incidents and a 12% increase in productivity.[8]

If we feel able to speak up with our opinions and believe that, when we do, those opinions are listened to and considered valuable, then we are more motivated. We are likely to *strive* and perform better, as is our organisation.

But time and again we come across situations where the focus on control and the rituals of so-called engagement undermine people's desire and ability to contribute.

The following is an example of this from Jeff, Head of Merger Integration in the advertising and social media world, who spoke to us about the merger of his specialist firm, let's call it 'SmallCo', into a larger parent 'BigCo'.

SMALLCO

In terms of employee engagement, the SmallCo people have moved from a world where engagement meant active participation in decision-making to one based upon merit badges, staff awards and nominees for employee of the month. For the SmallCo staff this is experienced as deeply infantilising, the equivalent of star charts stuck to the family fridge and used to reward children for doing their chores. Engagement workshops and staff briefings are viewed as 'a load of bullshit'.

In BigCo there is a deep-seated belief that motivation and engagement are in the gift of management. Years of scripted communication and 'town hall' (organisational or departmental wide, leadership-led) meetings, have attempted to keep everybody aligned and singing from the same hymn sheet. Consultation and involvement are a pretence, as is people's engagement.

It is only in knowing that we can speak up with our opinions, and that they are *genuinely* listened to and valued, that organisations can really build the engagement that is necessary to tackle the challenges ahead.

Only then will employees truly *strive* to perform better.

THE MORAL CASE

Most things seem to need a business case to get anywhere in our organisations. We need to prove our actions will lead to higher profits or operational efficiency. Changing habits of speaking and listening can indeed lead to these results, but they are also a matter of human potential, flourishing and dignity. This alone should compel us to focus our attention and ambition upon them.

Martin Buber, a twentieth-century philosopher, commented on the nature of our relationships with others and the world around us, describing two modes of encounter: I-It and I-Thou.[9] In the first, we interact in a transactional manner in order to get things done. Understandably and appropriately, we do a lot of that in organisations. But, says Buber, the problem comes when that is the *only* way in which we see and relate with one another. I-Thou signals a way of seeing and being with one another which is mutual, respectful, humane and recognises our shared experience and interconnection. It relies on our capacity to speak openly and listen to one another deeply. It is fundamental to our human being-ness.

In business and organisational terms this means seeing each other as fellow human beings first, and second as workers – there to perform a role. If we strictly confine our speaking and listening to the transactional, we silence ourselves and others. We restrict our conversations to the detached, phlegmatic, formalised and self-interested. We distance ourselves from the extraordinary experience of being compassionately connected with one another. In doing so we drain the colour from our lives.

A good example of this is our tendency to expel personal emotions from the workplace. Most of the time when a work colleague asks how you are, the reflex is to reply 'Oh, fine', even when inside you are feeling far from fine. In this way, the personal is taken out of the professional, which limits the capacity for rich connection and conversation.

If we aren't careful we find ourselves constructing a façade at work that is impenetrable. We create an environment – like the one in the science fiction film 'The Matrix' – where only certain things are shared and

MEGAN

Megan was asked how she was feeling a while back. At the time a close member of the family had been taken ill. There was no prognosis and no understanding of exactly how serious it was. Being someone used to 'fixing' things, Megan experienced this situation as extraordinarily anxiety-provoking.

At first she told no one at work. It did not seem appropriate, she wanted to protect the privacy of her family member and, critically, she didn't want anyone to think she couldn't cope.

Then one day a colleague asked her how she was. Megan paused and began by saying: 'Actually, I'm struggling right now.' Then she explained the situation. Her colleague stopped in her tracks, listened and later in the conversation, confided how she'd just had a breakdown that she concealed from her work colleagues.

Through speaking and listening to one another, the two of them uncovered their shared humanity. It feels almost sacrilege to turn it into a list of benefits, but it resulted in closeness, feeling understood, relief and warmth. Over the next few weeks, Megan spoke with a few more colleagues and in every case, they had a story they shared relating to their own anxiety or powerlessness. On most occasions, it was the first time they had spoken up in the workplace.

The conversations Megan had with her colleagues enriched her relationships with them, deepened her understanding of her experience and transformed the way she sees and relates with others more generally.

Yes, it happened that these conversations and patterns of support enabled Megan to stay functioning at work – there's a business case. However, that feels far less important than the deeper compassion and understanding she now feels for herself and for others experiencing anxiety and helplessness.

spoken about. Our conversations then primarily serve clinical execution of processes and procedures.

While of course it is appropriate to speak about some things in some environments and not in others, we need to keep an eye on our choices. These choices define the way we see ourselves and others. Restricting our conversations holds long-lasting consequences for our sense of fulfilment, purpose, self-respect, wellbeing and humanity.

OUR RESEARCH

This book is the culmination of decades of research examining how we talk, listen and learn with one another inside workplace systems.

Between us we have published half a dozen books examining organisational culture, change, dialogue, mindfulness and how it influences our relationships. Our research has been published in *Harvard Business Review* and numerous other global journals, magazines and online blogs.[10] Together we have many years of working in organisational development, executive coaching and leadership facilitation. We have heard the intimate details of the dilemmas, fears, strengths and shortcomings of leaders inside organisations across the public, private and third sector, in small start-ups and global giants.

In 2014 we began an extensive research project with Ashridge Executive Education, part of Hult International Business School, called 'Speaking Truth to Power'. We set out with these specific research questions:

- What happens when we make the choice to speak up or stay silent?
- How does an appreciation of the complexities of this choice inform effective leadership?
- How might individuals make more informed choices regarding speaking up?

A more thorough description of this research project is available in the appendix. In brief, we used the following methods:

- **Interviews:** We interviewed over 150 leaders in almost every industry you can think of: politics, law, finance, manufacturing, education, professional services, farming, civil service, charity, technology, health, education and defence.
- **Surveys:** So far, we have surveyed nearly 4,000 individuals across the globe and at all hierarchical levels, about their perspectives on speaking and listening up in the workplace.
- **Ethnographic inquiry:** This is the practice of participating in workplace activities, observing and interviewing people, gathering multiple (often conflicting) perspectives on speaking and listening up in specific organisations.
- **Collaborative inquiry:** This involves small group inquiry conversations held over a sustained period of years with groups of leaders, all

interested in altering the habits of conversations in their organisations, sharing what works and what doesn't.

- **Facilitating workshops:** We have tested, 'live', our emerging insights with hundreds of people, exploring what resonated and what didn't and how they could apply our research findings.

- **Personal inquiry:** As authors we have explored, with supervision, our own habits of speaking and listening to one another. We have examined the ironies of our method which relies on people speaking to us openly about their experiences of staying silent.

We understand the moments of speaking and listening up to be contextual. Therefore we do not attempt to unearth a formula that will predict whether truth is spoken or not. Rather our project is to understand the complexities inherent in these moments of choice. This enables us to make suggestions about how you can equip yourself to speak and listen in a way that is appropriate to the situation.

Our research is driven by a quest to help our organisations to be more humane, relational, ethical and productive and to help individuals within them to flourish. It is our hope that this book contributes to that.

ABOUT THIS BOOK

This book is made up of the eight chapters that introduce and then follow our TRUTH framework:

- **Chapter 1: Speaking the TRUTH in a world of power** explains the TRUTH framework in more detail and reveals how perceptions of power affect how we speak up, stay silent and choose who to hear.

- **Chapter 2: Trust: in your voice and the voices of others** asks why and when we do and don't have confidence in our own opinion and the opinions of others.

- **Chapter 3: Risk: how we experience it and how we create it** explores why speaking and listening up can feel risky for you and for those around you.

- **Chapter 4: Understanding: navigating the unwritten rules of politics and power** describes how our relative political power and our own agenda and that of other people influences who says what and who gets heard.

- **Chapter 5: Titles: how they give and take authority** uncovers how bias, entrenched in the way we label and categorise others, affects whose voices are heard.

- **Chapter 6: How to: speak and listen up with skill** advises how we can enable safer, more mindful, conversations.

- **Chapter 7: TRUTH in the future: the profound consequences of a digital world** is an exploration of how changes in technology may alter our conversations.

- **Chapter 8: Six compass points on the way to TRUTH** provides a summary of why speaking truth to power matters and what you can do to speak and hear truth better.

- **Appendix: Our research** includes more detail on our questions, methods and analysis. It lists available resources which offer additional support for you and your organisation in developing a better speak up, listen up culture.

KEY MESSAGES

- Speaking up and listening up matters in our organisations. Without it, you might only hear about misconduct and wrongdoing when it appears on the front page of the newspaper. It is vital for innovation and adapting to this latest age of upheaval. It is essential to motivation and engagement.

- Fundamentally, it matters to us as human beings. Through our conversations, we share, connect, empathise, seek support and offer it. We affect what others think of us and what we think of them. We learn what it is to be human. Without freely speaking and listening up, we live an emaciated life.

- Perceptions of power, status and trust rule how we speak and listen.

- Particularly in the workplace, we don't speak up or listen up very well. We tend to criticise others for their silence or for not listening, without examining our own abilities and responsibilities. We leave our own habits unchanged.

- TRUTH (Trust, Risk, Understanding, Titles, How-to), based on our extensive research, is a framework that enables us to improve our awareness of how and why we speak and listen up.

- This book aims to help you and your workplace flourish by enabling conversations to be more open, productive, compassionate and creative.

If you do only one thing now, take a stand on something you know people don't want to talk about, but you know is important. Think about how to raise it well and who to. Then do it.

NOTES

1. www.pwc.co.uk/services/economics-policy/insights/the-impact-of-automation-on-jobs.html
2. www.forbes.com/sites/forbestechcouncil/2018/03/01/14-ways-ai-will-benefit-or-harm-society/#67dae5f74ef0
3. www.managementtoday.co.uk/5-real-dangers-ai-according-experts/future-business/article/1457779
4. Higgins, J., Reitz, M. and Williams, C. (2017) The hero is head – long live the new hero! In *Inspiring Leadership*, Fleming, K. and Delves, R. (Eds). Bloomsbury, London, Chapter 3.
5. www.bbc.co.uk/news/business-44005844
6. www.reuters.com/article/us-volkswagen-emissions-culture-idUSKCN0S40MT20151010
7. http://news.gallup.com/reports/191489/q12-meta-analysis-report-2016.aspx?g_source=link_newsv9&g_campaign=item_223235&g_medium=copy
8. http://news.gallup.com/opinion/gallup/223235/create-culture-psy-chological-safety.aspxa
9. Reitz, M. (2015) *Dialogue in Organisations: Developing Relational Leadership*, Palgrave.
10. See www.meganreitz.com for a comprehensive listing.

CHAPTER 1

SPEAKING THE TRUTH IN A WORLD OF POWER

Perceptions of power affect whether we speak up or stay silent. They influence who gets heard.

In this chapter you will learn to use the TRUTH framework. It helps you understand the significance of power and enables you and others to speak up and listen up more effectively.

You will learn how to:

- talk explicitly about power and hierarchy to improve conversational effectiveness
- define power for yourself and assess its consequences on others
- follow our framework to analyse and improve your own conversational experiences.

WHAT DOES POWER MEAN TO YOU?

Examine the pictures below.

1. Think about your response to the word 'power'. Choose a picture that reso-nates most *immediately* with you. Don't dwell too much on intellectualising things.

2. Now choose a picture which most resonates with the way in which you perceive *your own* power inside your organisation.

3. Finally, choose a picture that portrays the way in which *your boss* uses their power to get things done.

Now look at the pictures you have chosen. What strikes you?

Do the images show a negative, neutral or positive view of power? Or a mixture of them?

OUR RELATIONSHIP TO POWER IS PART OF OUR PERSONAL STORY

Family experiences of power and authority greatly colour whether people are instinctively drawn to seeing power as a malign or benign aspect of life. Interviewing the CEO of a Teenage Crisis Centre, what emerged was a family background where only female authority was valued – and it took this CEO until well into his fifties to embrace those traits more often seen as masculine.

SIMON

We spoke to Simon, a thoughtful and intelligent executive in his fifties, who became angry when talking about what he saw as the outrages of the rich and powerful. In further conversations with him what emerged was an unresolved tension towards authority figures, particularly male ones, which he brought to life with the following story.

'My father had been in the military all his life and seen active service in some very nasty situations. When I was 16 (we didn't have the best relationship by then) he got me to lie on the floor. He wanted to show me how you can immobilise someone. He put his boot at the point between my skull and spine. He told me if I tried to move, my neck would break. I was terrified then and still am when faced with a particular form of male assertiveness – and can fall into the trap of denigrating and shaming so-called alpha males whenever I can.'

Sadly, a lot of people have family experiences that have exposed them or their siblings to mental or physical abuse – which in turn then plays out in an inability to engage constructively with people in positions of hierarchical authority. An appeal to people's rationality does little to address the heart-stopping relationship they hold with what it takes and costs for them to speak up to power. The ghosts of personal history cannot be wished away, although they can lose their intensity over time if properly paid attention to.

POWER AS A POSSESSION

In our personal stories and in many leadership development classrooms, power is often treated as a possession. Someone has it and someone doesn't. Someone has more than another person. Someone can give up a bit of power and someone can obtain more.

Apparently, you should aim to 'get' more.

We learn to categorise types of power. Positional power conveyed through job title. Personality power conveyed through things like charisma and behaviour. Expert power based on knowledge and skill. Social power based on connections, and so on.

This may be helpful in beginning our inquiry into power. However, power is *never* this simplistic.

SEEING POWER DIFFERENTLY

To become better at speaking up and listening up, we need to appreciate our own and others' complex, dynamic and subjective perceptions about what power enables us to do and how it constrains us. Take this story.

MEGAN AND THE NEW CEO

A few years ago, the business school that Megan is part of merged with another. For a period of time the political environment and the way things should be done was far from clear. The rules had changed but Megan wasn't quite sure how. She asked to meet with the new CEO because a couple of her colleagues had told her she really should do, both for her own standing in the organisation and to put her case forward in relation to what was important in the new combined school.

Waiting in the large and ornate coffee lounge for the new CEO to arrive, she felt somewhat nervous. Her thoughts were preoccupied with how important this meeting was for her and for those she felt she was representing. Without consciously articulating it, the new CEO felt to her to be comparatively powerful with a capacity to influence her professional future. 'I'm going to have to prove myself,' she thought. 'I'd better make a good impression,' she helpfully added to the list of pressures her internal narrative was busy telling her. This was to be speaking up as a performance in the face of power.

He arrived at the far end of the coffee lounge and paused to get a coffee. She quickly assessed what he looked like. Her mind worked like a supercomputer observing him and figuring out, with very little data, what he was going to be like. Suddenly he engaged with Julie, a member of the catering staff, in conversation and they both broke out in laughter. He stayed with her for a couple of minutes and they continued in their light-hearted conversation. Then he looked around, saw Megan and headed over.

With her mind still in overdrive, his encounter with Julie had recalibrated something – he appeared less scary and more approachable. He reminded her of a previous boss she'd got on with earlier in her career. She felt slightly more at ease and slightly less powerless.

They began to talk. She asked him about how things were going. He smiled and said: 'Well, it is quite daunting coming in as the CEO in a business school, trying to lead a group of leadership experts!'

▶

'Of course,' Megan thought warming to this man. She could imagine that would feel intimidating. In that moment she could see that her view of his power was constructed from her perspective only. But seeing the world through his eyes, his power was altered, levelled.

As they continued to talk, she continued to be curious about her shifting sense of their relative status and authority. It was far too simplistic to think of him as powerful simply because of his job title. In some ways, his status seemed elevated to her – his position, his previous experience and his network in the wider organisation. In other ways, it seemed contained and confined – he was new to this school, he was working now with a faculty of experts, he didn't know what he didn't know, he had a mammoth task on his hands to transition the two schools into one. At the same time, Megan went from feeling relatively junior to realising that she was one of the experts he was referring to. She had an influential network internally and he was probably aware that her story about him would be important in how he was seen. She felt the sense of her own power increase.

From this example you can see that our understanding of power is dynamic. It shifts according to the context we find ourselves in and as our perception of others and their perception of us changes. It is influenced by society and how we are brought up. This conversation happened between an American and a British national in the UK, and perceptions of power may well have been different if the conversation had been between Dutch and Chinese nationals in China. It might be different if one individual had had a life of privilege and the other had had a life of being in the minority and discriminated against.

To summarise then, in this book power is viewed differently to the simplistic notion of 'possession'. We define power as *socially constructed.* An essential and pervasive aspect of organisational life, it is not a thing or an objective possession which we can see, measure and all agree upon. Rather, power refers to dynamic and *subjective perceptions* that develop in relationship and change as a result of perceived status differences. These differences might relate to a combination of features such as hierarchical position, expertise, social connections, or simply because of gender, age, ethnicity or physical appearance. And our perception of all these features in turn is influenced by our situation, upbringing, cultural context, outlook and moment-by-moment sense-making *in relation* with others.

As human beings, we are, whether we are aware of it or not, constantly developing, constructing and negotiating power. Power has a major influence in determining who says what to who and what counts as true.

This means that we must bring our perceptions of power, in all their complexity, into view as individuals, organisations and societies. This can be hard, especially as it turns out, for those who feel powerful.

LIVING WITH THE SHADOW OF FEELING POWERFUL

A young woman arrives late at a meeting, fashionably dressed. The most senior person in the room, a man, greets her arrival with the words: 'Nice fuck-me boots'. Although there are a few in the room who look uncomfortable, nobody comments.

A nervous, newly promoted male executive arrives at his first board room meeting and is subjected to the banter of the rest of the team, teasing him for his unwillingness to get drunk with them the night before. They say he can't possibly fit in if he can't keep up on the drinking front. They think they are being clever and amusing. He experiences it differently.

When people are in contexts where they feel powerful, where they feel they belong and they have a right to speak their truth, they can become disinhibited. They can feel unconstrained in what they say. Bullying and harassment emerge when this is taken to extremes. In these cases, those in power are often more than aware of what they are doing.

However, people who find it easy to speak up are often *unaware* of what it feels like not to be occupying a powerful position that privileges what they say and how they will be heard. They assume that how they experience their own capacity to speak up must apply to everyone.

Admitting to the persistence of inequality can be difficult. When we raised it with a group of staff in a retirement community, they resolutely challenged whether there could be any advantage associated with ethnicity, gender or age because there was legislation to ensure discrimination didn't happen. At another time, during one of our major surveys, when we asked the question: 'Does someone's ethnicity or gender influence how you listen to them?', one respondent wrote that they found the question offensive. They wanted to wish away and disown discrimination. But that is impossible. Habits of privilege and discrimination are centuries old and take time and commitment to alter.

Power and its consequences are so often ignored or unseen, especially by those who have privilege. By pretending or hoping that organisational life is flat, that hierarchies can be disappeared and that as people we are free of unconscious bias, we miss the opportunity to skilfully speak up and enable others to in our social reality.

We miss the opportunity to thoughtfully consider how we might use our advantage to serve others and affect change.

POWER *OVER* OR POWER *WITH*?

It matters how we see our own power and what we see it to be in the service of. Sometimes we may feel we should use the power we perceive that we have *over* others – to direct and control. Other times we may feel a responsibility to use our power *with* others – to empower, enable and develop.

The founder of a famous firm of headhunters we interviewed is informed by the Rule of St Benedict, a Christian monastic order, that insists that the head of the monastery (or in this case the firm) listens to the youngest monk. As far as he was concerned, with the privilege of positional power came the responsibility to learn, respect and listen.

If we want to become even more skilled in speaking and listening up, we must have an appreciation of how power is constructed in relationships. We have to understand whether we construct and use power to control and confine, or to serve and develop.

Unfortunately our perceptions of power, and the assumptions we make as a result, are often unconscious. This means many of us have a blind spot regarding why we silence ourselves and especially how and why we silence others. Cultural habits develop in conversations which have defining consequences for us all.

BRUNO

Bruno, a colleague of ours, who worked in Nokia in its heyday, recalls being invited to meet one of its most senior executives, as all new joiners were. He was nervous and prepared all sorts of presentational material in order to demonstrate how busy and on top of his game he was. He arrived outside the executive's office and was immediately shown in; there was no waiting outside while the important person got on with their important work. The executive's desk was completely cleared of other activities, attention was firmly focused on this meeting and it soon was made plain that it was not Bruno's work he wanted to know about, but Bruno the human being.

The executive used his positional authority to grow Bruno's sense of personal significance within this new world.

POWER AFFECTS CONVERSATIONS, WHICH AFFECT CULTURE, WHICH AFFECTS POWER . . .

Organisations are not things that can be manoeuvred like a vehicle or made to operate with the predictability of a machine. If we want people to speak up more, telling them to do that, putting in a whistleblowing hotline, or circulating employee surveys are unlikely, on their own, to make much difference. These actions will not immediately result in people speaking openly, using the whistleblowing line or answering the survey in a thoughtful manner. Rather, they'll use them in the same way that established custom and practice says these sorts of formal processes should be used.

As our colleague Ben Fuchs, who spent many years working with conflict situations in civil society and organisations, puts it, power is the hidden magnet around which the iron filings of our various speak-up initiatives orientate themselves. If patterns of power stay the same, then patterns of conversational interaction stay the same – and the people who are the most powerful are often the least aware of the consequences of power. As with the COO Anthony, whose power meant that people couldn't tell him what they felt able and less able to say to him, he remained in a state of blissful ignorance.

Our conversations are created and made sense of through our subjective understanding of relative power positions which vary from moment to moment. We read the gestures and signals from others and adjust our perception of status and authority (even if we are doing this unconsciously). We then respond according to our new understanding. Our partner then reads our signals and the whole cycle continues: a never-ending dance of gesture and response where we cannot help but navigate relative power.

And here is the central point: workplaces are made up of people having conversations. Those conversations are influenced by perceptions of power. When our perceptions lead us into predictable conversational patterns and habits, we describe those customs and behaviours as culture. Culture then affects our conversations: whether and how we speak up – or silence ourselves, and whether we listen up – or silence others.

When we undertake to manage a culture change programme, we so often 'disappear' the enormous influence that perceptions of power will have on how we choose to behave and how our colleagues will respond.

'My door is always open,' we say. Then we wonder why no one comes through it.

'And have you got any feedback for me?' our boss says at the end of our newly introduced 'continuous performance management' meeting. With a sharp intake of breath our mind races with all the things we *could* say, then settles on: 'No, things are going really well . . . mmm . . . all good . . . '

Changing habits and cultures cannot occur unless we have a way of understanding what's going on in our conversations. We have to see more clearly the choices we have and then make different ones.

To help, we have developed a framework called TRUTH. It aims to bring power into view and identify and expand our choices. It aims to enable us to be more skilful at both speaking and listening up.

THE TRUTH FRAMEWORK

We have spent years inquiring, with hundreds of others in many sectors and geographies, into what happens when we make the decision whether to speak up or stay silent. We have examined how we decide we are going to listen intently to another person, or do something that might silence them.

In the introduction we gave you an overview of the TRUTH framework. We listed the five questions that we often navigate in these moments of choosing whether to speak up and listen up. Let's look at this in a bit more detail noting how our sense of power shapes what does and doesn't get said. Conversations are, of course, always made up of speaking up *and* listening up, but to help get to grips with what is going on we are going to break it down into the two major components (even though we know they are intertwined).

First, let's look at it from the point of view of speaking up.

THE TRUTH ABOUT SPEAKING UP IN A WORLD OF POWER

Picture the scene. You are a female non-executive who has just joined the all-male board of a major services industry. As you delve into the paperwork in order to understand the business as quickly as possible, you notice that their tax affairs, while legal, are clearly taking advantage of various loopholes in the law. You are surprised and think that there is the risk of reputational damage if the press were to examine the financial dealings more closely.

At your first board meeting, a discussion on financials begins and you pause. Here it is. The moment of choice. Do you say something? Do you express your concerns?

We interviewed this non-executive, let's call her Susan, and she explained what went through her mind, which we describe here alongside the TRUTH framework:

- How much do you **T**RUST the value of your opinion?

  Susan was checking in, asking herself: 'Do I have something relevant and coherent to say?' 'Am I sure this is an issue?' 'Is it important?'

'Do I know what I'm talking about?' She was fairly sure that what she had spotted was important and yet she was new to the industry and the organisation. Perhaps she didn't really understand what was 'normal practice'. Perhaps others knew best.

- What are the RISKS involved in speaking up – or not speaking up?

  Susan focused in on the likely consequences of speaking up and found herself considering in particular: 'How will I be perceived if I bring this up in this first meeting?' 'What will they think of me?' 'Will I look stupid if I'm wrong?' 'Will I jeopardise the relationships with these critical people right from the start?' On the other side, and lower in volume, was the question: 'What level of risk do I think there is for the company if I *don't* speak up?'

- Do you UNDERSTAND the politics of who says what to who . . . and why?

  She glanced around the table trying to read the signals between the members of the board. 'Is this the sort of challenge that is okay to make in the board meeting?' 'Whose toes will I step on if I say something?' 'What are the rules in this group about what gets spoken about and how?' Figuring out the politics, personal agendas and ego needs in any group can be tricky, let alone a group that you have only just joined.

- Are you aware of the TITLES and labels others attach to you and you attach to others – and how that shapes what you can say in your conversations?

  Susan was acutely aware of the labels she felt were being applied to her – two in particular – 'female' and 'new'. The gender disparity in the room was resoundingly obvious to her and her newness even more stark, given that she was the first female non-executive this organisation had ever had. In this board room 'new' and 'woman' felt lower status. She felt she was under the spotlight and her opinions may hold less weight. She was also busy labelling the CEO and finance director in particular – 'male', 'confident' and 'expert' – and these elevated their status and power in her eyes, simultaneously adding to the risks of speaking up and getting it wrong, whatever wrong meant.

- Do you know HOW to choose the right words at the right time in the right place to the right person?

  Susan ran through various scenarios of how she could challenge the tax affairs, but the uncertainty surrounding the politics and the people around the table meant she felt she just didn't know what to say or how. The conversation swiftly moved on before she had time to feel comfortable with how and what she would say.

Susan stayed silent. Soon afterwards the press got hold of the tax dealings of the organisation. The story dominated the front pages of the papers. The public outcry seriously damaged the reputation of the organisation and the board and, by association, Susan.

Of course, Susan didn't work through the TRUTH questions systematically, or even consciously at the time. When we find ourselves in these moments of choice we focus on particular questions and not others. We've interviewed some people who seemingly never question the value of their own opinion – it's *always* valuable as far as they're concerned. Some are oblivious to the political environment that they are in and so it doesn't feature in their choices. Others are consumed by the potential risks of speaking up – they can hardly think of anything else but the consequences – which paralyses them.

We are *not* suggesting that the five questions in the TRUTH framework are exhaustive, discrete, static or of equal weight, but they do seem to reflect the common concerns that tip us towards speaking up or staying silent. The framework therefore should be considered as a useful aide memoire rather than gospel.

Take a moment to consider something that you would like to speak up about – perhaps some feedback, or an idea. Maybe it's something that you've been mulling over for a while, something that you've wanted to bring up but have always filed away in the 'too difficult' or 'not sure how this will land with others' box. Now walk your way through the TRUTH framework and some of the subsidiary questions that come with it. If you're serious about it, it might help to make some notes:

1. How much do you really Trust the value of your opinion? What are the voices inside you that make you doubt your contribution? How many of them are relevant to who you are now (often voices of doubt come from way back, from a critical parent, a bad teacher or an unskilled boss)? How is the context that you want to speak up in making you believe in, or doubt, yourself?

2. What are the Risks of speaking up about this specific matter? What's the worst you could imagine happening? What's the worst that could actually

happen? What's the upside? What are the risks of keeping silent? What steps can you take to manage the risks and rewards?

3. Do you Understand the politics? Whose toes might you be treading on? Who might be your allies? How does your agenda fit with that of powerful others? What are the sources of your power in this context and how can you make good use of them?

4. How are the Titles you are putting on people, and they are putting on you, helping or hindering you in saying what you want to say? How can you work with, rather than wish away, the conscious and unconscious biases of how people will treat you – whether you like it or not, whether it's fair or not?

5. How do you need to phrase what you say? What are the words that will land well with people? How do you speak so you'll be heard? What balance of advocacy and inquiry will be most effective? How much certainty or doubt in your tone will work best? Is this something best spoken up about formally or informally, on the record or off the record?

The TRUTH framework helps you think through whether and how to speak up. It also shines a light onto an area which many of us are less aware of: how we invite others to speak and listen to what they have to say.

THE TRUTH ABOUT LISTENING UP IN A WORLD OF POWER

Now let's turn our attention to the other component of any conversational exchange, the quality of the listening. Speaking up only has meaning if listening up is happening at the same time. Paying attention to how people, especially ourselves, are listening up is a vital aspect of conversational discipline and one we tend to overlook in comparison to the time invested in learning how to speak up well.

Catherine glanced round the table at her new colleagues. It was the first day as the new CEO of a large manufacturing organisation and she was with seven of her direct reports. So far things had gone smoothly. In fact, that was the problem. They had gone far too smoothly and far too politely.

She had made a few observations, challenged and suggested a couple of changes. These had all been met with nodding heads of agreement and quiet acquiescence. Little by little, she began to experiment. 'How far can I go before they argue back?' she wondered.

It seems she was able to go very far indeed. No matter how extreme a view she put forward, her new team agreed.

Here's what she thought was going on, using the TRUTH framework for listening up:

- How much do you **T**RUST the value of others' opinions?

  Catherine knew that her organisation's success, and therefore her own, depended upon having a leadership team who came up with original ideas and who weren't afraid of challenging the way things were done. She knew she had a very experienced team and she wanted to know what they thought. She very much made this her top priority in her first few months.

- What are the **R**ISKS involved when others speak up to you?

  She was surprised at her team's initial silence but she spent some time trying to understand their world. She came to understand that her predecessor was a renowned bully and if people challenged him they usually disappeared shortly afterwards. It was going to take quite some time for her team to shift away from the habit of staying quiet for self-preservation. As far as they were concerned, speaking up meant they would lose their job or at the very least be sidelined.

- Do you **U**NDERSTAND the politics of who says what to you . . . and why?

  If you wanted to be successful in the old regime, you agreed with the CEO and you competed with your colleagues for recognition and resources through separate one-to-one clandestine conversations with the CEO. In those encounters you presented your world in a distinctly rosy light and the world of your colleagues in a considerably less positive way. These were the rules of survival and it had created a highly politicised environment. Catherine realised that she was being presented with a particular view on reality – a highly censored one.

- Are you aware of the **T**ITLES and labels others attach to you and you attach to others – and how that shapes what you get to hear?

  The title 'CEO' in this organisation conveyed significant power and status. Along with it came a whole list of assumptions and expectations that included 'the CEOs view is correct', 'don't challenge the CEO' and 'don't, whatever you do, tell the CEO the truth'.

- Do you know **H**OW to help others to speak up?

  Once Catherine had come to understand the dynamic described above, she came up with a creative way to change the habits of conversation. She brought a red card to her leadership meetings and each member had a turn in holding the card for the duration of that meeting. If you had the card, your job was to challenge any decisions that the group made – you had to play devil's advocate. The members experienced this as intensely uncomfortable at first, but gradually over time they got used to questioning and realised that nothing bad happened to them as a result. Within a couple of months the red card was no longer needed – challenge was just a natural feature of the conversation.

Take a moment to think of someone whose point of view you would really like to hear and who you very rarely, if ever, hear from. Perhaps you want some unfiltered feedback, or suspect there's an idea that's being stifled. Or maybe the data you're getting is too good to be true, or seems to be suspiciously coherent and tidy.

Now walk your way through the TRUTH framework and some of the subsidiary questions that come with it. You might want to make some notes.

1. Do you *really* Trust the value of their opinion and want to hear from them? Or are you actually looking for an opportunity to bring them round to your thinking? Are you more of a power *over* than power *with* sort of person? What is it that you want to hear from them – and how will you avoid 'leading the witness' so that it becomes a game of them second-guessing what you want to hear?

2. What could be the real and imaginary Risks this person has about speaking up to you? How do you dial down the imaginary ones and reduce the power shadow of any formal authority and influence you have over their future in the workplace? What are the risks to you of shifting the nature of your relationship with this person? Could your authority be enhanced or reduced by changing your way of engaging with this person?

3. Do you Understand your own politics, agenda and priorities? Do you understand their agendas and priorities? How explicit do you both need to be with each other?

4. Are you able to work with the unconscious and conscious biases that come with the Titles you put on each other? How might you under- or over-value what they say?

5. How does this conversation need to happen? Where and when would put the other person at their ease? What are the words you need to use that will be heard as an invitation to speak?

WORKING WITH TRUTH

Our TRUTH framework is intended as a useful lens to engage with topics too often ignored or wished away. It is meant to stimulate conversations, *not* to provide a universal template that will allow truth to be spoken to power.

How the framework gets used within an organisational context is in itself a very interesting piece of data. If the top team decide that this is for everyone else, but not for them, that says they have a limited understanding of how speaking up and listening up works in practice. They are absenting themselves from paying attention to the role they play in creating a particular speak-up, listen-up culture, reinforcing a habit that speaking truth to power is about them and not us.

We have been working with individuals, teams and organisations on their TRUTH and through inquiry and reflection seen how their choices around speaking and listening up become clearer.

We want you to be clearer on your TRUTH. That will serve you and your organisation's ambitions. But it will also serve your fellow human beings.

KEY MESSAGES

- Power drives who says what to who, who gets heard and ignored. You can't escape it, it's often not fair – you have to live and work with it.

- The way we see power is influenced by our personal story and our relationships with powerful others as we grow up, starting with our family experiences.

- Power is often seen as a possession. However, it isn't static or objective. It comes alive, is constructed and changes in the moment between people. It is ready to become a force for progress or personal growth, or a means to control or to bully others.

- You choose your relationship with power and affect how it shapes what you do and don't say. Power may be inevitable, but how it shows up for you is not.

- Those who are seen as powerful are often those least likely to see and empathise with what it's like to feel powerless. If we are from a privileged majority group, it is extremely difficult to remember that things we take for granted, such as the ability to speak up and be heard, are not that easy for others.

- Our perceptions of power influence our conversational habits: who speaks up and who gets heard. When these habits get stuck into patterns, our workplace culture emerges. In a symbiotic way, culture then affects who speaks up and gets heard.

- TRUTH (Trust, Risk, Understanding, Titles, How-to) is a framework that enables us to improve our awareness of how and why we speak and listen up.

If you only do one thing now, think of someone who may have felt silenced by you in the past (perhaps because they perceive you as powerful). Give them the experience of being heard next time you see them.

CHAPTER 2

TRUST: IN YOUR VOICE AND THE VOICES OF OTHERS

This chapter will help you understand when and why you speak up, confident and trusting in your own opinion – and when you silence yourself because you're not sure. We will help you reflect on why you sometimes listen and why, at other times, you silence others because of judgements you make, consciously or unconsciously, about the value of what they have to say.

You will learn:

■ why trust is at the heart of speaking up and listening up

■ how to hear your different inner voices and which ones can sabotage you

■ to see how power affects who you speak up to and whose opinion you do and don't count

■ to catch your 'superiority illusion' in the act – those times you feel you're pretty damn good and any problems lie with everyone else

■ how the way you think of yourself dictates how and when you speak up and listen up

■ how to build confidence in your own opinion and the opinion of others.

If we don't trust in the value of *our own* opinion, we are unlikely to say anything. If we don't trust in the value of *others'* opinions, we are unlikely to listen. Trust is the ignition for speaking up and enabling others to do the same.

Trust is also contextual rather than binary. Some of us generally trust and value our own opinion more than others do, or listen to others with more interest, but trust is not something you simply have or don't have. We all tend to value our own opinion more in *certain* contexts, about *certain* subjects, with *certain* people. And we value the opinions of *some* people, when they talk about *some* things at *some* times, more than others.

SPEAKING UP – TRUSTING *OUR OWN* OPINION

Do you have something to say? Trusting in our own opinion means we:

- believe we have a genuine contribution to make
- know what we feel strongly enough about to speak up about.

Our survey data indicates we have a high degree of self-belief in the value of our own opinion. 82% of respondents said they nearly always or usually believe they have a genuine contribution to make and 84% knew what they feel strongly enough about to speak up about (at the time of writing).

But if we don't feel our voice will make any difference to the situation, think we are being put through some nominal consultation process, aren't that bothered about the subject matter or simply have more important things to be getting on with, we are less likely to speak up.

Let's look at the two statements above in turn.

BELIEVING WE CAN MAKE A CONTRIBUTION

IAIN

Iain is a project manager at a major healthcare company based in Switzerland. He works at the headquarters alongside 10,000 other employees. Many issues relating to wellbeing, communications and culture are debated and decided upon by the leadership team. As part of its commitment to being inclusive and representative, the team advertised for a 'Gen Y' employee (born in the 1980s or 1990s) to have a seat at its meetings. Iain applied and got the job.

▶

Surrounded by more senior people (including his boss's boss) who were experienced, direct and assertive, Iain had to find his voice. He struggled at first but knew his perspective was different and important – he had experiences on the ground with employees that others around the table couldn't have because of the positions they held. To begin with he tended to listen to others and leave with 'the thoughts still trapped inside', going home frustrated.

At dinner with his mum and girlfriend he talked it through, concluding he needed to trust his opinion more and speak up because he had a genuine contribution to make. Gradually he built up his confidence, forcing himself to speak up at every meeting, and choosing a subject on the agenda he felt he could most contribute towards. He found a mentor, a member of the leadership team, who encouraged him and gave him feedback on the way he spoke and the impact he had.

One day he read a blog, written by a senior leader at the company, describing how in her team meetings they nominated a 'truth teller'. This person would be expected to productively challenge and bring up subjects that were being ignored, avoided or missed. This story inspired Iain to nominate himself the truth teller for the leadership team meetings he attended.

He trusted he had something of value to say. The label gave him the courage and commitment to speak up.

Consider the meetings you participate in at work. Perhaps some are with people junior to you and some senior; some might be finance-based, others more strategic or people-based; some are squarely in your area of expertise, while others are more peripheral to what you know about.

1. In which meetings do you feel confident to contribute?
2. In which do you question yourself more?
3. What are the conditions when you feel you do or don't have something worthwhile to say?
4. Is it just down to expertise – or are other things also at play?

Part of the context that helps us believe we can make a contribution comes from being given the necessary information. We came across some striking differences of approach here, such as in sharing financial information and equipping people to make sense of it. In his start-up company Dimitri made sure that everyone in the company, largely made up of ex-automobile sector factory workers, knew how to read the accounting books. He gave them the freedom to speak as they saw fit in the financial context. However, once the company was then bought, this financial information went into the control of the acquiring firm's finance department. It disappeared from sight, along with the employees' confidence in speaking up.

1. Are you given the information you need so you feel like you can make a contribution?
2. Are you given the time and space to digest information so you can speak up well?

KNOWING WHAT WE (AND OTHERS) FEEL STRONGLY ABOUT

In most workplaces there are assumptions about what people *should* feel strongly about. We were recently involved in supporting an American hospital going through a major restructuring and wanted to explore how people outside the executive suite felt things were going. It proved hard to get time with anyone, but then we sat down with the director of nursing. 'What you have to understand,' he said, 'is that the vast majority of people here earn less than $25,000 a year. They come in, do a job and at the end of the day they're tired and want to go home. They've seen it all before and just don't have the capacity to care about the questions you're asking about the new structure.'

DAN

Dan worked at a children's charity and was passionate about its work. Going through the finances one day he discovered the CEO was syphoning money out. Dan felt he had no other option than to speak up. The case went to court and he was thrust into the public eye as the scandal hit the headlines. The stress devastated him and his family. Tragically, his pregnant wife lost their baby, with stress a major contributing factor. Their marriage buckled under the strain.

We asked him whether, knowing the consequences, he would do the same again. His immediate answer was 'No way!' Then he paused, looked terribly torn and said 'But how could I not?' His values, sense of integrity and care for the work of the charity meant that he could not fail to speak up.

Our work has shown us how easy it is for senior people to miss what *really* matters to ordinary workers. A CEO told us she and her executive nodded through a two-day delay in people getting paid in order to get a new IT system up and running. On the day it was announced, the CEO came upon one of the cleaning staff in floods of tears. A two-day delay meant missing payments. Default and personal disaster loomed because this cleaner lived on a knife edge. A two-day slippage in payment meant everything to the cleaner but nothing to the executive who had no understanding of how precarious the finances were for the families of the poorest people who worked there.

People's capacity to feel strongly at work reflects where they are in their life. Annika has been selling services and kit to the law enforcement and security industry for twenty years. Her boss froze her out of a recent bid and as a result mistakes were made and a $1.5m contract was lost. It was clear the responsibility for the loss lay with her boss, the head of global sales. But he had a track record of failure and had never suffered any consequences. Annika just didn't have the energy to go public with the issue. In two years' time she planned to leave anyway, to join her husband in a new business venture. For now she just needed to keep her earnings steady and even with this lost business she'd still meet her targets.

Unlike Dan, Annika had no sense of moral outrage to stiffen the sinews, this was just normal business life where sometimes 'shit happens'. If Annika had seen herself having a longer-term career with the company then maybe she'd have said something. But why rock the boat when you've got better things to do with your life?

1. What do you have the energy to feel strongly about at work?
2. What is going on in the rest of your life that makes workplace issues more or less important?
3. What do people around you actually feel strongly about? And what's going on in their lives?
4. How much energy is diverted into people pretending to feel strongly about what they've been told they *should* feel strongly about?

WHO ARE YOU? ARE YOU THE SORT OF PERSON WHO SPEAKS UP?

When we consider speaking up, one question we navigate, often unconsciously, is 'Am I the sort of person that speaks up about this in this situation?' Dan spoke up because he could not live with himself if he didn't – he was the sort of person that could not let this sort of wrongdoing go by unchallenged. Annika was more world-weary and less invested in the ethical integrity of her workplace.

In the list below, choose three labels that describe most strongly the sort of person you think you are:

Adventurous	Dominant	Open-minded
Ambitious	Easygoing	Opinionated
Articulate	Enthusiastic	Patient
Brave	Fair	Persuasive
Calm	Genuine	Principled
Caring	Honest	Proactive
Charismatic	Inquisitive	Quiet
Clever	Insightful	Responsible
Competitive	Kind	Sensitive
Confident	Logical	Tolerant
Creative	Loyal	Tough
Determined	Meticulous	

The way we describe ourselves provides us with a compass that guides our choices in our conversations. When we hear inappropriate comments from a colleague who thinks they are being humorous, when we see someone else being discriminated against, and when we have an idea, we ask ourselves whether we are the sort of person to speak up about this. The titles and descriptors we hold in our heads about ourselves can urge us on or silence us.

What implications do your labels have on how and when you speak up?

Every label will have a strength and a weakness, a time when it helps and a time when it hinders. If I see myself as calm, for instance, there are many occasions when it can help in conversations. By being calm I might invite people around me to speak more calmly, and so allow conversations to be more reasonable. But calm is not a universal strength. Sometimes emotional energy is essential if people are to know what it is they or others care about. Without emotional charge, human beings can't make choices – because we lack the data about what matters. On the other hand, if all we had as a label was 'enthusiastic' then we'd need some calm to temper that enthusiasm from time to time – unfettered enthusiasm is likely to exhaust every conversation in the end, with no time for reflection and digestion.

When you think about the labels you are willing to own about yourself, consider the following:

1. What are the strengths of these labels when it comes to speaking up and listening to others?
2. What happens when I overplay this label? What are the unintended consequences of me seeing myself (or others) in this way? Who gets silenced? Who gets heard?
3. Which of these labels are more about the role I'm in and the status I have than who I am as a person?
4. How skilled am I at working with my portfolio of labels so I can bring different qualities to bear at different times?
5. How good am I at sharing my labels with others so that we can play to our collective strengths in a conversation?

ARE YOU AN IMPOSTER?

Despite the positive traits you believe you possess, do you ever have thoughts like these at work?

- When are they going to find out I don't know what I am talking about?
- I shouldn't be in this role – others would be much better.
- I got lucky – I don't deserve this success – and I should have done even better really.
- I'm probably going to mess this up.

If you do, here's the good news – you are not alone. Up to 70%[1] of us experience this psychological phenomenon called the imposter syndrome: a persistent perception that we are inadequate despite external evidence to the contrary.

Even highly successful individuals suffer from imposter syndrome doubt. Maya Angelou, the poet, writer and civil rights activist, said, 'I have written 11 books but each time I think "Uh-oh, they're going to find out now. I've run a game on everybody and they're going to find me out".'

Sheryl Sandberg was COO of Facebook, number one on the Forbes list of most powerful women in technology and worth over $1 billion, when she publicly admitted to feeling like an impostor: 'There are still days when I wake up feeling like a fraud, not sure I should be where I am.'[2]

Some of the world's foremost consultancies and law firms have said that they recruit 'insecure' over-achievers as these people will often work above and beyond, for perhaps the wrong reasons, in a constant effort to prove themselves to themselves and others.[3] In her book, *Leading Professionals,* Professor Laura Empson quotes a law firm managing partner as saying, 'Partners are earning over £800,000 a year and the average guy here will be thinking, "God, I'm not worth it".'

Self-doubt can, of course, be good – keeping us grounded. If you have no doubts at all and a grandiose sense of self, you could be labelled a psychopath[4] (and a disturbing number of business leaders might fall into this category[5]). The philosopher Bertrand Russell wrote: 'The whole problem with the world is that fools and fanatics are always so certain of themselves, and wiser people so full of doubts.'[6] But sometimes the imposter voice gets too loud. It drowns out the voice that gives us confidence and we silence ourselves.

In our work with executives, imposter syndrome shows up in a number of common situations:

- **When we've just been promoted into a new, stretching role:** We're in the first meeting with our new team and find ourselves thinking: 'What do I do now?' We wonder whether the positive image we transmitted in the recruitment process was possibly a bit far-fetched.

- **When we are in the minority:** A new-in-post, female, non-executive director found herself around the table with an all-male board. As they asserted confidently using jargon only someone who'd been at the company for years could master, she had to work hard to overcome the voice that questioned whether she had anything to contribute.

- **When we perceive others around us to have higher rank due to experience, hierarchical position, personality or confidence:** Our tendency is to defer to their higher power – 'They must know better than me'. In his work on 'rankism', Robert Fuller[7] argues that senior people are endlessly involved in status games, seeking to ensure others feel in a lower-status position, and so prone to feeling like an imposter.

- **When we are challenging the norm or speaking up in opposition to other powerful voices:** Sticking with the dominant discourse or agreeing with powerful others can often feel like the safer path to take. To challenge a norm can be hard work for you and for others.

It often requires people to step out of their automatic patterns and into a slower way of talking things through. This can feel difficult (even wrong) in the face of senior people who want to get on through a busy agenda quickly and efficiently.

1. When have you heard or not heard the imposter voice?
2. What conditions typically lead you to question your capability?
3. What are the implications for whether or how you speak up?

VALUING YOUR OPINION TOO MUCH

Even if we recognise the imposter voice all too well it is still likely there are times when we rate our opinion too highly – sure of our rightness. If we are voicing our opinion too much it can hold us back just as much as the imposter voice.

One habit that leads us to voice too much is the belief that the best way to lead is to offer advice and solve problems for everyone else. The COO of one of the world's largest investment banks told of his habit of walking the trading floors, wanting to be helpful by making suggestions. He now realises he was an active nuisance, getting people to do lots of unnecessary work.

Believing that we are an expert at everything because of our senior position is not a recipe for *constructive* speaking up.

Speaking up well requires the courage to say something but also requires the skill and wisdom to know when to stay silent and listen, or when to ask a question rather than advocate an answer.

ARE YOU BETTER THAN EVERYONE ELSE?

We asked nearly four thousand managers whether they thought junior-, middle- and senior-level employees at their organisations would speak up about misconduct, challenge ways of working or offer ideas. Then we asked them whether *they* would.

The following table shows the data at the time of writing. The percentages indicate how many respondents felt that the group in question would usually nearly always or always speak up.

On average, across all data, 50% of respondents believe junior employees would usually, nearly always or always speak up about misconduct. They would speak up less often with ideas and less still with challenges to

Who speaks up about what?

	Junior employees	Middle-level employees	Senior employees	You (respond-ents)
About misconduct	50%	67%	73%	82%
Challenge ways of working	27%	52%	68%	70%
Offer ideas	40%	63%	72%	81%

ways of working. Overall, the perception appears to be that middle-level employees speak up more often and senior-level employees even more so.

But look at the column labelled 'You'. This refers to how often respondents said *they* would speak up. It would appear that they are far better at speaking up than everyone else in their organisations.

It is possible that this reflects the 'superiority illusion' – believing we are better at something than we actually are. Research indicates that although leadership talent is, statistically speaking, normally distributed, 80% of leaders think they are better than average.[8]

So while we must not over-inflate the imposter voice, we must simultaneously have our hand on the volume control of our superiority voice.

HOW TO TRUST IN YOUR OPINION MORE

We have been talking so far about how we believe (enough, but not too much) in our own opinion so that we can speak up. Here are some ways people we interviewed and surveyed have strengthened the trust in their opinions, enabling them to speak up more effectively:

- **Prepare well:** In the work we do with individuals seeking to improve the way they speak up, we draw on the expertise of actors. They get people to rehearse speaking up to maximise their impact. Once they have done it a few times they feel more confident in what they have to say. One Royal Shakespeare Company director we interviewed expressed amazement at the lack of rehearsal and preparation people do prior to conversations that matter to them in the workplace (and at home). Our confidence to say something tends to increase if we have a plan in place.

- **Look for opportunities:** A non-executive director explained how he scans the agenda and paperwork for upcoming board meetings with an eye to looking for opportunities to speak. He suggested looking for subjects that either you know you have a useful perspective on, or that you feel strongly about, then preparing to talk to those points in the meeting.

- **Start with 'small elephants':** It can be trickier to speak up with something that runs counter to the dominant discourse. If you want to step into more controversial areas you might want to start with the small elephants as one of our interviewees described it ('elephants in the room' being subjects people know about but ignore, usually because they are politically sensitive). Research at Ashridge Executive Education found that stretching ourselves, giving something a go, was the most important method for developing leadership.[9] Starting with what's manageable and learning as we go means we can continue to break new ground and develop skill in speaking up.

- **Be mindful of your inner imposter voice:** Notice when your imposter voice rears up and engage with it – be curious about it rather than try and turn it off (which is tricky to do). If it's saying 'I won't do this as well as others', reflect on times when you have spoken up effectively and remind yourself what you know about doing that. If it's saying 'You're not as good as others', remind yourself what you do bring to the table and the perspectives you have that will be different to others. There is more on this strategy later when we talk about training ourselves to be more mindful in conversations.

- **Don't contribute to the swirl:** Iain, who we interviewed at the Swiss healthcare organisation, had a lovely phrase: 'Don't contribute to the swirl.' He regularly checked in with himself about what he chose to speak up about. Were they issues where he had a contribution to make? Or was he scoring political points or pursuing his personal agenda? We say many things to portray ourselves in a good light, position others in a worse one or please people we feel are powerful. While some of this is inevitable (and sometimes appropriate), speaking up and feeling good about why and how we do that means sticking to genuine contributions and not adding to the swirl.

- **Get an ally, coach or mentor:** Knowing you're not alone can make things a lot easier. Too often we can see ourselves as lone agents in the world, whereas we are always part of some wider system. Understanding how to engage with that wider system, and who else can support your ideas and opinions, takes the burden off you as an isolated individual. It removes that sense of needing to be a standalone hero. An ally can support you when you speak up, while a coach or mentor can help you prepare and give you the honest feedback about how you are and are not speaking up.

- **Learn from mistakes:** When we experiment with speaking up it's likely we'll 'mess up'. We might say something we didn't mean to. We may upset someone. How we cope with failure is an integral part of how we learn and develop. Michael Jordan, the basketball megastar, says in a Nike commercial: 'I've missed more than nine thousand shots. I've lost almost three hundred games. Twenty-six times I've been trusted to take the game-winning shot and missed. I've failed over and over and over again in my life. And that is why I succeed.' Success and skill in something cannot happen without failure. Meeting failure with self-compassion is an integral aspect of learning and continuing to experiment.

LISTENING UP – TRUSTING THE OPINIONS OF OTHER PEOPLE

Interviewing over 150 senior leaders we noticed a pattern – nearly all focused, at least at the beginning of conversations, on how they spoke up. They talked about the valuable things they had to say and about how others made it difficult for them. Most needed nudging to talk about how they listen to others and how they invite *others* to speak up by valuing those opinions.

In fact, in a diagnostic we have been using, our respondents report that they value their own opinion around a third more than they value the opinion of others. In some teams we found people value their own opinion between two and three times more than that of others.

It is all very well focusing in on how we speak up in our workplace, but if we are not also focused on how we listen up we will all end up talking into space.

Let's now explore how we value *other people's* opinions, the necessity of discernment and the danger of silencing others.

To trust in the value of others' opinions, it helps if you are:

- open to having your opinion changed
- aware that your perspective is partial and limited.

If you can't do either of the above, it probably means your capacity to value others' opinions is restricted. In reality it won't be a yes/no answer. It is likely that you are *sometimes* open to having your opinion changed – and sometimes not. You are probably aware only *sometimes* about *some areas* where your perspective might be partial.

Commonly, we listen up when certain others talk about certain subjects. Our radar picks up opinions on subjects about which we are engaged and interested. Then there are subjects we are simply not aware of or believe we know enough about and don't need others' views on.

Some of the things that get in the way of us being open and interested in other's views, include the way in which we:

■ assume whose opinion counts, and whose doesn't

■ stick to the same group of people when we seek opinions and perspectives (a form of confirmation bias leading us to hear only the things that fit with our views)

■ perceive that we are better at listening than others

■ overplay the voices of powerful others, and underplay the voices of those less powerful.

We will look at each of these in turn now.

ASSUMING WHOSE OPINION COUNTS

HARVEY

Harvey, a CEO, told us passionately how diversity mattered to him. How he wanted his team 'to bring their whole selves to work' and speak up. Everybody's opinion counted.

Then Harvey paused and said: 'But I do have my little list – of those who fit and those that don't.'

When seeking opinions, despite intentions to listen well to all team members, he was referring to his 'little list' to determine whose opinion counted and whose should be discounted.

And here's the thing: we *all* have a little list. Our capacity as human beings to discern who to listen to and who not, who to focus on and who not, who is safe and who is not, is an evolutionary in-built process that is very useful to us.

But as many of us continue to regard ourselves as good at listening, we fail to check and challenge how we comprise our little lists.

Are there some people who, when they come into your office (if you're lucky enough to have one), make you sit up, ready to hear what they have to say? Are there others who elicit a response more akin to resignation or frustration as you see them come towards you? And then are there those who you just don't really see because you are distracted or simply apathetic towards?

Just to emphasise how we might assume different values in different opinions, consider the list below.

Who would you presume might have an opinion that is more valuable? We are not asking you for a politically correct answer here about what *should* be the case – just what you notice is your default assumption:

- Junior employees versus mid-level employees versus senior employees.

- HR versus operations versus sales versus finance versus IT.

- Someone who has been at your organisation a long time versus a new joiner.

- A part-time worker versus a full-time worker.

If 'it depends', what does it depend on and what do you notice about your assumptions?

STICKING TO WHO WE KNOW

In our survey, we asked hundreds of people in the workplace whether they tended to seek out the same person or group of people when needing opinions or advice. Two thirds say they usually, nearly always or always do.

This is neither surprising nor bad. There is a lot to say for being discerning in whom we listen to. Many of us also know who in our network will 'give it to us straight', and who might not, so it makes sense to seek these people and perspectives out.

However, as with the little lists that we hold, we benefit from examining who we tend to go to and perhaps more importantly who are left out from our inner sanctum of privileged voices.

Even when we do seek to bring in alternative voices, we must then ask ourselves whether we are *really* intending to listen well to them. In one interview we came across an interestingly perverse attempt to engage with difference. The responsibility for representing an alternative point of view in a hierarchical institution was given to the most junior member of the team. This immediately ensured that it lacked the weight that came from being a senior insider.

1. Whose perspectives do you miss out by favouring certain people's voices?
2. What is it that makes you comfortable with certain people and not others?
3. If you could diversify just a bit, who could you include?

ASSUMING WE ARE GOOD AT LISTENING

Let's return to our research data. We asked how well our respondents thought senior employees in their organisations listened when other employees spoke up about misconduct, challenged ways of working and offered ideas. Then we asked how *they* would listen to others.

The table below shows the data at the time of writing. The percentages indicate how many respondents felt the group in question would usually, nearly always, or always listen up.

Who listens to what?

	Senior employees	You (respondents)
About misconduct	72%	93%
Challenge ways of working	43%	91%
Offer ideas	50%	93%

On average, across all data, 72% of respondents believe that senior employees would usually, nearly always or always listen up about misconduct. They listen somewhat less to ideas and less again to challenges about ways of working.

Now look at the column labelled 'you'. This refers to how often the respondents said they would listen up. Surprise, surprise, our respondents are *far* better at listening up, it would seem, than senior employees in their companies.

So what is going on here? The superiority illusion again perhaps? We find that our self-concept generally is higher. We are fine – it is everyone else that is the problem.

Needless to say, this view cannot be correct in all cases. Not everyone can be better than everyone else. The first step in listening up better is to reflect rigorously on when, where, to whom and about what we tend to listen to and when, where, to whom and about what *we don't.*

OVERPLAYING THE VALUE OF THE OPINIONS OF POWERFUL OTHERS

JOHAN

As with the story of the investment banker COO who walked around offering advice, trying to be helpful, we often gift the opinions of the powerful too much weight. As a young(ish) management consultant working for a prestigious US-based consultancy in the 1990s, Johan had a responsibility for compiling an internal directory of subject matter experts (this was in the pre-internet era). This directory would enable consultants to get hold of best practice knowledge quickly. They would be confident that what they were hearing came from the very best in the company. It soon became clear that the 'knowledge directory' had an uncanny resemblance to the firm's management hierarchy.

The value of someone's opinion was a function of their formal power and position. This was despite the firm doing a lot of work in areas where it was highly likely that younger employees would have better first-hand knowledge – the emerging use of the internet being a good example. Despite senior managers often being unaware of what was actually being done with clients on the ground in fast-moving industries, they were assumed to be the go-to people.

UNDERPLAYING THE VALUE OF THE OPINIONS OF LESS POWERFUL OTHERS

A colleague tells a story of a workshop he ran for a senior leadership team of a global pharmaceutical company. After a tea break the finance director was late back and the work of the group delayed. As the FD made his reappearance, the CEO was heard by all to say: 'Dollars waiting for dimes.' A throwaway line, probably meant to be humorous, but brought about by some frustration, that spoke to how he saw the importance of his contribution compared to the FD.

We came across a story from one marketing executive who was working in an insurance company looking to redesign its basic product offering. Customers were shown the product in focus groups and said it was rubbish. On hearing this, the most senior executive in the room's first instruction was along the lines of: 'Find me the idiots who brought these idiots in!' His assumption was that he knew better than the customers. Indeed, he felt his opinions were of more value. In time he eventually calmed down and realised that they had indeed over-complicated the product.

We often like to think we listen to those we perceive as less powerful or lower down the hierarchy, but when they say things we don't want to hear are we still listening?

HOW TO DEVELOP TRUST IN THE VALUE OF OTHERS' OPINIONS

Here are some ways our interviewees suggested you might enable yourself to be more open to the opinions of others – while remaining discerning:

- **Remind yourself why others' opinions are important:** This underpins everything. To acknowledge the limits of personal knowledge can be difficult. To accept we need others, challenging. However, as the business and moral cases set out in the Introduction attest, listening to diverse views is vital for our own success, the success of our team and our organisation. The 'iceberg of ignorance', reputedly developed by Sidney Yoshida, found that 100% of front-line problems were known to the front-line employees, but only 74% were known to team leaders, 9% to middle management and just 4% to top management.[10] When we find ourselves in senior roles we can know comparatively little of what is going on at the sharp end.

- **Nurture curiosity:** What if we held the question 'How can I learn from this person?' rather than 'What should I tell them?' This is a major shift in most of our professional training, where advocacy skills are greatly over-developed compared to inquiry skills. To develop curiosity means creating the space for, and valuing, open inquiry in meetings – and avoiding the popular habit of crowding them out with content and lectures. In our work with family mediators, we keep on being reminded that in a conversation we can only own half the meaning – and talking at people more doesn't change that. Being curious is an essential requirement if we want people to do more than go through the motions of agreeing with us.

- **Be mindful of your 'little list' and question it:** Notice discounting as it happens. Our little list will be built around people whose opinion we think counts and who speak in a way we prefer. One senior interviewee spoke of their preference for people who could 'be brief, be clear and be gone'. They'd had to teach themselves to be more tolerant of those who needed to do their thinking out loud and didn't necessarily take the most direct route to what they wanted to say.

■ **Seek out new voices regularly:** Finding ways to engage with people who are usually overlooked is essential. One hospital CEO made it a priority to spend time with the nightshift – people who are otherwise simply not seen. An air force commander instituted a policy of always being driven by the youngest cadet on the base as he toured the country. The rule was: 'What gets said in the car, stays in the car.' The youngster would speak to what was on their mind and the commander could get a feel for what life was like at the bottom of the pyramid.

Too often attempts to meet with groups in different hierarchical roles turn into 'ask the boss' exercises, which invite those higher up to go into answering mode. A better approach for these sessions might be to see them as 'tell the boss' exercises.

■ **Spend time getting to know the reality of others:** A senior sergeant in the police force was hard-wired to have empathy for his junior police officers. When we asked him how he stayed in touch with the reality of their lives he said: 'Easy. I join them on the beat'. He didn't get in the way of their work but helped by providing an extra pair of eyes as they patrolled the streets either on foot or by car. As they spent some hours together he was able to pick up on what was said, how it was said and what was left unsaid. Too often, as our investment banker COO noted, the only reality that senior people know is what gets put into the official reports. In the case of the banking industry prior to the crash of 2007/8, this banker felt that it was only the most senior people who believed what was being officially reported.

■ **Catch our default reactions:** We most easily silence people when we react rather than thoughtfully respond to what has been said. A Canadian CEO told us of her negative reaction to people who brought her bad news. She'd grown up with an angry mother – if someone, including her, said something challenging, her mum would respond punitively. The CEO had unwittingly learnt to respond like this herself but, recognising this, had learnt to let that initial reaction wash through so her adult self could respond constructively to challenge. Authenticity and spontaneity are not the same thing.

Speaking up can't happen unless we trust in our own and others' voices. However, trust alone might not be enough. Next we will explore the risk and consequences that we perceive are at stake through speaking up or staying silent.

And if the risks are too high, even if we trust in our opinions and those of others, nobody speaks.

KEY MESSAGES

- You have to learn to trust and value your own opinion.
- You are more likely to speak up if you know that you have something to contribute and if you are clear about what issues you feel strongly about.
- You will feel like an imposter sometimes, silence yourself and make mistakes when you speak up – that's normal.
- You have to learn to trust and value the opinion of many others – not just the usual suspects.
- If you are not open to changing your mind or if you fail to see your perspectives as partial and limited you are less likely to value the opinion of others.
- Your character and how you like to think of yourself, drives how you speak and listen to others.
- You might sometimes fall into the superiority illusion, believing you are better at listening up and speaking up than others. This could lead you to blame others, wait impatiently for *them* to change rather than take responsibility yourself.

If you only do one thing now, notice when your imposter voice speaks and remind yourself of your strengths and abilities.

NOTES

1. https://www.tci-thaijo.org/index.php/IJBS/article/view/521/pdf
2. http://www.telegraph.co.uk/women/work/imposter-syndrome-why-do-so-many-women-feel-like-frauds/.
3. https://www.ft.com/content/ba0c9234-a2d7-11e7-9e4f-7f5e6a7c98a2
4. https://www.forbes.com/sites/amymorin/2016/01/30/5-surefire-signs-youre-dealing-with-apsychopath/#37bc4e7262f6
5. https://www.forbes.com/sites/victorlipman/2013/04/25/the-disturbing-link-between-psychopathy-andleadership/ and http://www.bbc.com/capital/story/20171102-do-psychopaths-really-make-better-leaders

6. Bertrand Russell in his 1933 essay 'The Triumph of Stupidity'.
7. https://www.huffingtonpost.com/robert-fuller/somebodies-and-nobodies-u_b_264283.html
8. https://hbr.org/2017/03/how-to-tell-leaders-theyre-not-as-great-as-they-think-they-are
9. http://tools.ashridge.org.uk/website/IC.nsf/wFARATT/Experiencing%20leadership/$file/ExperiencingLeadership.pdf
10. https://corporate-rebels.com/iceberg-of-ignorance/

CHAPTER 3

RISK: HOW WE EXPERIENCE IT AND HOW WE CREATE IT

Speaking up happens when we trust in what we have to say and are willing to accept the risks of saying it.

You may think to yourself 'I have something to say.' Your next thought though is likely to be ' . . . but what will happen if I say it?' This chapter is about risk and how our perceptions of the consequences of speaking up affect what we say – and what others say to us.

You will learn:

- what it is that scares you about speaking up and how you can understand and mitigate the consequences

- how to catch yourself catastrophising and get a sense of perspective

- how your cultural perspective on power influences how you perceive the risk of speaking up

- how processes and forums in your workplace may disregard power differences and therefore lead to silence – or allow only politically safe and familiar views to be presented

- *who might find you scary*
- *how you can create safer spaces where others can speak more freely to you.*

SPEAKING UP – THE RISKS YOU PERCEIVE

WHAT ARE YOU SO SCARED OF?

Simon is now in his early sixties and is the chair of a medical charity. At the age of 21, as a young medical student, he witnessed a surgeon's malpractice. When he spoke up, he was ordered into the consultant's office: 'Young man, if you value your future career you will desist in this right now.' Without doubt the message was 'speak up and lose not only your job but your career'.

So he stayed silent. And it still haunts him.

In our interviews, we have come across individuals who have faced severe consequences as a result of speaking up. Dan, the whistleblower, faced tragedy. The CEO of an educational organisation in the UK who we interviewed, lost his high-profile job when he decided to 'tell the Minister – and then the press – straight' about what was going on in the assessment of school children's exam results. Victims of sexual harassment face very real risks to their physical safety, of being ostracised, condemned in the press and losing their jobs[1] if they speak up.

However, most of us silence ourselves day to day because we are worried about two more seemingly mundane reasons. We don't want to hurt or embarrass others. And we want to be liked.

OTHERS MIGHT GET HURT . . . OR WILL THEY?

This is a story we have told in many of our workshops.

MIKE MASSIMINO

Mike Massimino is a former NASA astronaut. He explains that, while spacewalking, astronauts need to put the visor on their helmets down when the sun passes to protect them from the sun's glare, and up when they move into darkness. As the shuttle orbits the earth, astronauts experience 16 sunrises and 16 sunsets in a 24-hour period. So they may need to put their visor up and down a few times.

▶

> *At the end of a seven-hour spacewalk at the Hubble Space Telescope, Mike needed to untether his safety harness but he had forgotten to put his visor back up when he entered darkness. Not realising, he thought his near blindness was because he was about to die. It was only when he got back inside the shuttle and noticed his reflection that he realised his mistake.*
>
> *As Mike reports,[2] his colleague, Drew Feustel, said to him, 'Hey, I noticed you had your visor down at the end during that last night pass.' 'What!' Mike said. 'Are you kidding me? You noticed that and never said anything? I couldn't see a thing, I thought I was passing out or dying! Why didn't you say anything?'*
>
> *Drew replied, 'I didn't want to embarrass you.'*
>
> *Mike said: 'Didn't want to embarrass me? Wouldn't it have been worse if I messed up my safety tether transfer and floated away into space?'*
>
> *'Good point,' Drew said. 'My bad.'*

We need to feel that we belong to a group and are safe by being part of the gang. Embarrassment is our modern social reaction to the threat of exclusion.

But it isn't just the fear of embarrassing someone that silences us. We worry about upsetting them and then being perceived negatively as a result. Think back to an occasion where you knew something about a colleague, maybe a peer or your boss, which was holding them back at work. Perhaps you noticed that they frustrate others with the way they talk or listen to people. Perhaps you heard them make a comment which they thought was humorous but was in fact discriminatory. Or perhaps you thought the way they dressed was inappropriate. But you didn't tell them.

Maybe, at some point, you have stood by and witnessed casual racism or sexism. Perhaps you listened into and even joined in with gossip which you knew was likely to be biased, incorrect or unfair. It is likely that you did this because you worried that calling it out would lead to *you* being perceived negatively and rejected.

Even though we know our feedback could be extremely valuable, we don't share it. Because the thought of seeing the other person shocked or upset, or the prospect of them getting angry and defensive with us and possibly blaming us, is just too much to bear.

In these sorts of situations we live in hope that someone else might speak up. We try and convince ourselves that somehow the person will discover this information by themselves.

In our survey, fear of upsetting others and fear of being perceived negatively come out as the most common reasons for staying silent.

Protecting our relationships and being accepted by others really matters to us all.

THERE'S NO POINT

Megan was working with a group of middle managers at a major European bank. The discussion kept running into the sand, coming to a halt because of the impenetrable belief that speaking up was pointless. The group was convinced that nobody was listening. The perceived risk here was simply that if you spoke up, nothing would happen – and then you'd face disappointment and frustration.

In our survey we asked respondents what they expected to happen if they spoke up about various things. As you can see in the table below, over a third of respondents felt that if they spoke up with a problem or risk, they would be ignored and one quarter felt they would be suppressed (prevented from speaking up). A third felt they would be ignored if they spoke up with an idea and about one in six thought they'd be suppressed.

Will they listen if I speak up?

	Problem/risk	Idea
It is likely I will be ignored	39%	36%
It is likely I will be suppressed	25%	17%

With statistics like these it is hardly surprising many of us conclude there is little point in speaking up.

IT WILL JUST RESULT IN MORE WORK

Have you ever been in a meeting and had an idea or realised that something needs to be done, but decided to stay quiet because if you do speak up the response from your boss might be 'What a great idea, why don't *you* go and implement that and let us know how it goes?'

With many of us feeling maxed out already, the last thing we need is yet another project to lead or opportunity to develop. And others might not thank us if our idea leads to more work for them.

If we think a new boss, a restructure or a change in direction is in the offing, we may conclude there is no point in speaking up and rocking the boat because everything is bound to change anyway and we'll end up doing double the work.

We work with the health and social care sectors in the UK. Everyone knows that if they think systemically and explore the connections between the services then the system as a whole would deliver better outcomes for the communities they serve. But the amount of work required to challenge the current reality, where each unit is fiercely evaluated against short-term unit specific targets and objectives, feels significant and politically risky.

THE RISK OR REWARD OF NOT SPEAKING UP

The risks of speaking up are often ringing in our ears. When there's also no obvious reward for speaking up or compelling rewards for staying silent, it is likely that we will do just that.

LUIS GARICANO

In a visit to the London School of Economics in 2008, the Queen asked senior economists why no one had seen the financial crisis of 2007/2008 coming.

Professor Luis Garicano[3] responded that indeed many had seen it coming, but 'those working at every point in the lending chain were eager to continue doing the job they were paid to do: mortgage agents generating loan requests in exchange for a nice commission; banks granting the loans they knew they could package and pass on; rating agencies giving high ratings to products they could not understand. . . on dubious assumptions based on 12 years of data; and, most worryingly, asset managers (pension funds, etc.) buying these securities because if they did not, they would underperform their peers and risk being fired'. There was a clear advantage in keeping things as they were and a clear disadvantage in speaking up in order to change a system that was bringing in huge bonuses.

Rewards for speaking up often appear small to non-existent so they are often outweighed by the risks of social and professional exclusion.

Back to our survey. Here's how likely speaking up about a risk or problem or offering an idea would result in reward, punishment or support.

What will happen to me if I speak up?

	Problem/risk	Idea
It is likely I will be rewarded	20%	30%
It is likely I will be punished	15%	5%
It is likely I will be supported	67%	70%

Speaking up with a problem or risk is unlikely to gain you a reward. While most thought they'd be supported, there were still a third of respondents who felt they wouldn't be and a not insignificant 15% thought they'd be *punished.*

In railway infrastructure work we were told that, it's not in a site leader's interests to report near misses during track maintenance and repair work. There are no tangible incentives to do so and the ensuing investigations result in over-runs, missed targets and lower bonuses for them.

Respondents were slightly more optimistic about the prospect of speaking up with an idea – and yet still the majority felt reward was unlikely and over a quarter felt it unlikely they would be supported.

So why speak up if there's nothing in it for you? Perhaps it is easier to just assume someone else will do it, pass the buck, or in a world of constant churn, leave it up to whoever comes after you.

IT'S NOT MY JOB

Doubtless some in the lending chain prior to the financial crash of 2007/8 thought what they were doing was wrong but believed that it was not their job to speak out. So often we stay silent because 'Someone else is bound to say something if I don't' or 'It's not my job to say anything'. 'If there's something wrong then the regulators should find it or the CEO needs to say something.' In some situations, this can be a valid belief, but in others it is a wonderfully easy way to abdicate responsibility.

JOE

We interviewed Joe who told us that in the mid-1990s he attended a team-bonding event in Amsterdam. At the time he was one level of seniority below being a full partner in the firm. A full partner who was at the event decided that it would be fun for the whole team to go out into the town's infamous red light district. The fact that the team included a number of young, junior women didn't cross his mind. The evening went ahead and everyone seemed to join in with the fun of walking through the district and observing the sex trade in action. A few days later Joe's immediate boss called him into her office.

One of the young women had reported to her how uncomfortable the evening had been and how she had felt unable to challenge the partner. 'Did you do anything to challenge the idea of going into the red light district?' Joe was asked. Shamefully he hadn't, preferring to stay silent and go along with a course of action despite being in a position to challenge what was being proposed. He reflected that he had been hiding behind a habit of deferring to senior people, failing to see it as his job to challenge them (despite being the person best positioned to do so in this case).

WHAT HAS EXPERIENCE TAUGHT YOU?

> What has happened to you when you have spoken up previously? What happens to others around you when they speak up?

Experience will have introduced you to a wide range of consequences and coping strategies.

There might be the time you embarrassed yourself, or caused embarrassment for others, by saying the wrong thing at the wrong time. The times you stayed silent and let things unfold, even though you knew your silence was part of the conspiracy. The times you sat on a message because you couldn't see an easy way to pass it on to those who needed to hear it. Maybe there have been times you have spoken up and have been ignored.

BILLY

We were recently asked to help a professional services firm improve transparency. We interviewed many people and listened to the stories that they told about speaking up. Some of these stories had reached almost mythical status – having been told again and again. Their accuracy was certainly in doubt, but they mattered because they affected perceptions of risk.

One interesting story apparently happened about seven years ago when a staff member called Billy had challenged the previous CEO publicly in a meeting. About two weeks later, Billy was nowhere to be found, having exited the company rather swiftly.

Seven years ago this happened. With a previous CEO. And Billy may have left for personal reasons. But the story that kept being repeated was that if you challenge upwards you could expect to be fired.

'Smoking shoes' was a phrase we heard used in two other organisations we worked with. The cartoon-like image being that people disappeared so fast after challenging the boss that all that was left was a pair of smoking shoes. Again, the truth of the events that underpinned the story was hard to tell, but what is true is that the story lives on and people stay silent as a result.

Our experiences and the stories we hear (and often retell) affect our perceptions of risk. They might not bear any semblance to reality. But they do affect our choices, very often leading us to imagine catastrophic outcomes.

CATASTROPHISING

Although the risks of speaking up can be very real, we also have the tendency to overinflate them – catastrophising about what might happen if we say anything.

MARK

Megan was running a workshop with a leadership group from an international retail organisation. Mark, in his late twenties, was the youngest there. He was seen as high potential and had been at the organisation for the last eight years and seen it grow exponentially. He had been promoted at a similar rate as his boss, with whom he had worked for the entire period.

▶

The organisational culture was 'work hard, play hard and don't complain – just do it'. As a result, Mark put on a brave face for the first two days of the programme. It was on day three in a private conversation with Megan that he admitted to being close to breaking point. He was recently married and had a new baby, but wasn't seeing either his wife or his little girl nearly enough. He was now facing an ultimatum from his wife – spend more time with the family or risk a divorce.

Inquiring into why he wasn't sharing his predicament with his boss, Mark described his thought process like this:

1. If I say something, my boss will think I just can't handle the pace.
2. Then he will assume that I won't be able to perform in the future like I have done previously.
3. He will stop giving me challenging assignments.
4. So in the next promotion rounds I will be passed over in favour of others who are prepared to put the hours in.
5. If I don't keep progressing I will be the next in line for losing my job in the restructuring that seems to happen on a yearly basis.
6. If I lose my job, I will never manage to get another one that offers me as many opportunities as this one.
7. I will earn less, plateau and not be able to provide for my family in the way I want and need to.
8. My family will be disappointed in me and I may lose them as a result.

Mark had gone from 'if I speak up' to 'I will lose my family' in the blink of an eye. He found himself in no man's land. Ironically, if he said nothing he'd lose his family, but if he did say something the same result would happen.[4]

Talking it through we examined the assumptions he was making. A big one was that performing well and putting in long hours are inextricably linked – that there was no way of working differently to reduce his hours and still be regarded as a high performer. Another was that his boss would see him as a complainer and incapable if he mentioned the importance of work–life balance.

We worked out that the evidence for these assumptions didn't stack up. We planned his conversation. He had it and his boss helped him to figure out a different work pattern and put in more resources where needed.

WHAT YOU CAN DO TO MANAGE RISK

In an analysis of our research diagnostic, the number one area of concern was how little respondents felt able to manage the risks of speaking up, with less than half feeling they knew how to do this well.

Here are some suggestions from the people we have interviewed about recognising risk, realistically, and then mitigating it:

- ■ **Talk things through and plan what to say:** This makes the risks often seem (and are) lower. Mark, the young father mentioned above, worked with an actor on the programme and practised exactly how he'd tell his boss. He received vital feedback on what he was saying and how he was saying it that made the constructive outcome he got more likely.

- ■ **Learn how to challenge and give constructive feedback effectively:** It is a skill that *can* be practised and learnt and there are ways to do it that make it more likely that what you say will be well received. The All Black's New Zealand rugby team offer one another feedback beginning with the phrase 'permission to enter the danger zone!'[5] When you are saying something challenging to a 115 kg, 195 cm tall All Black, you want to give them a chance to prepare themselves to receive it in a productive manner. Later we give you tips on how to speak up effectively in more detail.

- ■ **Be clear about your intentions before you speak up:** If the other person can really see and believe that you are speaking up with *their* best interests in mind, then the risk of a negative response reduces. It can help to spell out your concerns. A colleague of Megan's started a recent conversation with: 'I am worried that I won't say this in the most skilful way, but I really want to help – will you forgive me if it doesn't come out quite right?'

- ■ **Find an ally:** There is something to be said for safety in numbers. If you have something challenging to say, it can help to have a few allies who also think the same and are willing to speak up with you. You might be heard better and it can take the spotlight off you.

- ■ **Notice when you are ruminating:** This is when you catastrophise about risks and consequences that are unlikely to happen. Write down your thought process (similar to the way we described Mark's earlier on). Then look back at it and highlight your assumptions. Then systematically examine the evidence for each assumption. We will explain more about how you can learn to notice your thoughts, and rather than be swept along by them, question them and see the assumptions within them.

■ **Ask yourself what your responsibility is:** Too often we leave it for others to say something. We take the role of bystander. Yet we feel better about ourselves if we act with integrity.

LISTENING UP – HOW *OTHERS* PERCEIVE RISK

POWER BLINDNESS

Power and risk surround us, day to day, in our workplaces. However, the risks of speaking up and the art of creating safe ways for people to speak up are often not discussed. Those of us who are seen as powerful (even if we are blind to it) forget what it's like to be less powerful in the system. We wonder why others aren't offering ideas or challenging as much as we want them to.

We ask them to speak up. We tell them our door is always open. We miss the irony in our words: 'I don't want any yes-men around me. I want everyone to tell me the truth – even if it costs them their job!', so Samuel Goldwyn, the American film producer, purportedly said.

A colleague of ours told us how the CEO of a European industrial giant he had worked for was informed that he needed to become consultative and engage with people more. The CEO held a town hall meeting, where he stood centre-stage, said his piece and then asked people for questions. No one said anything. The CEO left the stage and said (his actual words were a bit stronger): 'Well that was a waste of time.' He is a powerful, confident and well-resourced man. Yet he has no idea of what it takes for people to speak up in such a setting.

WE FORGET HOW SCARY WE ARE

Who do you think finds you scary? Who might think twice – or maybe many more times – before they say something to you?

If you responded to these questions with thoughts of 'nobody!' or 'hardly anyone – I'm really approachable' then you would be similar to many of the people we have interviewed and surveyed.

Think again.

This is the biggest blind spot we've uncovered. Many of us believe we are approachable – and indeed we *are*. However, it is inevitable that other people apply titles and labels to us. We might be able to do very little about some of these, but they could mean certain people will think we are scary or inaccessible.

For example, which of these titles and labels might be applied to you (even if you disagree with them yourself)?

Leader

Manager

Confident

Influential

Liked

Connected (has a good network)

Attractive

Tall/physically well-built

Clever

Quick-thinking

All these labels, and many more, can make others wary of talking to you if they convey status and authority. There's nothing right or wrong about it. It's just what happens.

We've found that many organisations put the onus on the less powerful to speak up to the more powerful. They run training programmes aimed at middle managers that include 'How to have courageous conversations'. Too often the most powerful groups absent themselves from such development work, forgetting that their scariness is perhaps the biggest factor that keeps others silent.

FRANCOIS

Megan had been coaching Francois for a few months with a view to him getting promoted to managing director. She received a call one day from him, delighted that it had just been announced that he'd got the job. 'But the only thing is,' he said, 'they announced it two hours ago and ever since then I've watched as people exit my office.' He explained that his colleagues, some of them once peers, seemed suddenly reticent in speaking to him in the same ways as before, now that he held the title of MD.

Francois realised what was happening, but many of us are blind to our own power. Discounting it means we lack the empathy necessary to realise others find speaking up to us risky.

In our survey, 66% of respondents thought that junior employees would 'never' or 'rarely' find them scary. It would appear that respondents thought the prospect of more senior people finding them scary was very unlikely – 80% thought this would never or rarely be the case.

> Which colleagues might find you scary?

APPRECIATING CULTURAL ATTITUDES TO POWER

History is littered with stories about what happens when we don't take perceptions of power difference seriously. A hierarchical culture in Korean Airlines may have significantly influenced a fatal crash in Guam in 1997 and similarly in Columbian Airlines in a 1990 New York crash. In both instances, questioning authority was culturally unacceptable. Co-pilots were scared to speak up and challenge,[6] even to the extent of facilitating their own death and that of everyone else on board.

Our cultural upbringing and experiences colour our assumptions about whether it is typically risky and unacceptable to challenge someone senior, or whether they're fair game and the risks are minimal. In conversation with Maurice, a Canadian leadership development expert, he told the story of how in Hong Kong he was shocked when his students explicitly stated that one of their goals in life was to show respect for their parents. Being of a Freudian turn of mind, he expected people to be much more North American and focused on achieving independence from their parents, with self-actualisation as the primary ambition. It took his local Hong Kong colleagues to bring to his attention how much longer the Confucian tradition had been in place compared to the Freudian one.

But it can be difficult to spot one's own cultural orientation and see it as a perspective – rather than right. It is not possible to objectively label cultures – they are always *in relation* to one another. As Erin Meyer observes in her work on culture,[7] a Dutch employee may consider Mexican team members as relatively hierarchical, whereas a Chinese team member might consider the Mexicans as relatively egalitarian.

1. How does your cultural context influence your assumptions about speaking up?

2. In particular, do you automatically assume it is okay for those more junior to you to challenge you? If you do, you may underplay the risks that some experience (particularly if they are from different cultures) in speaking up to you. You may consider yourself approachable, while forgetting that your more senior labels means you aren't.

OUR FORMAL SPEAK-UP PROCESSES PRETEND WE ARE EQUAL

As the example of our frustrated European CEO at the town hall meeting shows, the forums and processes we create to ensure conversation happens across hierarchy, cultures and departments can naively disregard power differences.

When we acknowledge that some might find it risky to speak up, we introduce whistleblowing lines, 360 reviews, anonymous employee surveys and suggestion boxes. Yet these are far from infallible and there are more pitfalls perhaps in instigating these processes and then assuming they solve the issue.

Consider the debacle at Barclays when the CEO tried to find out the identity of a whistleblower.[8] Or the not-for-profits organisation our long-standing colleague Michael worked with: the three most senior executives realised that people would find it difficult to ask direct questions to them at a town hall meeting, so they sat on a stage answering anonymised questions sent in beforehand. One question stumped the three of them and so after the meeting they managed to track down who asked the unanswered question and gave them an answer. This provided employees with proof that there was no anonymity and that asking anything difficult will get you tracked down (however well-intentioned the tracking down is).

Have you ever paused before entering the demographic data on an employee survey?

A senior executive in the mental health sector we know won't fill in online surveys about organisational culture because the demographic data at the start means he knows the CEO will be able to identify him – and she has a track record of not wanting to hear bad news.

Megan recently worked with the HR director of a European utilities organisation, designing and delivering a workshop for senior managers. The theme was 'stepping up to lead' and in particular, how to enable dialogue in their teams. The CEO was scheduled to spend an hour with them. The first suggestion from the HR director was that the CEO could talk about what he thought the group needed to develop in order to be effective leaders and then he could answer questions about the firm's strategy.

> How many times does this sort of meeting happen in your organisation?

Megan pointed out that this 'ask the boss' format was somewhat ironic given the themes of the workshop. She suggested that the CEO reflected on what he would most like to ask the group – what he was most curious about learning – and start and finish the conversation from there. For many senior executives this is much harder work than simply turning up and delivering a well-grooved script. In fact, the HR director's first response was that it would take too much time to prepare.

CREATING SAFE SPACES AND PROCESSES

Creating safe places to speak up is often the gift of the more powerful. We have seen how tricky it can be for power to be taken seriously – by those who are perceived to have it. Organisational processes, such as town hall meetings and open-door policies, can amplify people's sense of insecurity and be received with cynicism.

However, we have interviewed many leaders who have carefully considered what it takes and have developed forums that work.

A base commander said he was going to be sitting in the canteen at a set time but no one came to see him. Through experimenting, he discovered the time to listen was on a Friday evening in the sergeants' mess when he could join in more informally and people would open up. He talked of having to wear a flak jacket because people would jab him in the chest so much as they made their point. The safest place to speak to him from below the sergeant rank was for his driver, the most junior cadet, to talk on the long journeys they took together.

During a major restructuring of a government department, the new structure was presented over Skype to everyone involved for 15 minutes. Then the Skype call was shut down for an hour as people were given the opportunity to discuss the implications of the announcement in their home teams. Then an hour later a spokesperson for each team asked questions when the Skype call recommenced. This allowed employees the time to understand the information and gave them a chance to ask questions collectively, both of which reduced the perceived risk of speaking up.

In a hospice we studied, a senior nurse, when told of a mistake with giving drugs, responds to staff by lightly saying: 'More paper work for me!' She knows that making a drug mistake is very upsetting for her clinical staff. She knows she has to take the heat out of the situation, by turning it into a bureaucratic issue, before having a conversation about what can be learnt and done. Her hospice relies on staff speaking up about mistakes, so they have to carefully navigate how they respond to convince staff it is okay to talk about these things.

Visual methods, which in some circumstances are perceived as less threatening than spoken English, are being used by a number of leaders we interviewed in order to gather feedback. For example, a children and young adults mental services unit have a technique that they use with their clients that they also use in their own internal appraisal process called 'Talking Mats'[9]. This uses interactive picture symbols to make communication more collaborative and co-creational. In John's work with Cardboard Citizens, a homeless person's theatre company, he used a technique called 'Blob Trees',[10] involving pictures presenting different emotions. This allowed people who often didn't speak English to express their emotions in a way that works for them. It was regarded as a safer, less intimidating process.

LISTENING WITH RISK IN MIND

If you want to enable others to speak more openly to you then you have to appreciate the world from their point of view, particularly how they may perceive status, authority and safety. Here are a few suggestions from our interviewees:

- **Step into their shoes:** This is easy to do superficially, but harder to do deeply. Considering these questions can help:
  - What sources of power might others perceive you to have?
  - If there were to be risks that they perceive, what would they be (regardless of whether you think they are realistic or not)?
  - How maxed out do the people you're talking to feel? How can you make it okay for them to raise issues without fear of getting even more overloaded?

- Are others shying away from offering ideas or identifying problems because you always ask them to sort it out or implement it? That *may* be what is appropriate and what the other person wants, but it may not be.

- **Open up effective informal and formal forums:** Write down all the different groups of employees (and perhaps customers, suppliers and partners) and list the ways in which they currently get hold of you and communicate with you. Consider how it might feel for them to speak up at these events. For example, notice if the forums for one group of employees tend always to be large group ones. Might this feel risky for people to speak up at? Notice which groups of employees have no direct access to you and then how easy or risky they might perceive the other communication routes, such as surveys or 'up the chain of command', to be. Map out what would be more effective.

- **Notice the signals you send when others speak up to you:** Do you receive their comments with interest? Do you thank them? Some of us have default patterns when others disagree with us, or raise challenging issues, and we need to focus on regulating our emotions, particularly if we feel threatened by something someone says. How have you treated those who have spoken up to you in the past? We discuss this in more depth later: the signals you send today will affect how others consider the risk of speaking to you tomorrow.

- **Proactively invite constructive challenge and initiate debate:** Don't wait and assume employees will say what they think. Ask skilful questions that make it easier for others to talk to you: 'If there were to be a different perspective on this issue what would it be?' 'If there was something that I hadn't spotted that might get in the way, what would it be?' 'If you were a customer, supplier or another employee, what issues would you see with this?' 'If there were to be one thing I could do differently, what would it be?' Use (in moderation) outsiders who can say the unsayable. We will nearly always want to blame the messenger who brings news of difference, so better to work with this reality than wish it away.

- **Give people the time to think through things and the opportunity to collectively give feedback:** It reduces their fear of speaking up and you get better information. It gives people the opportunity to respond rather than just react to news.

- **Take steps to reduce power difference:** Make others feel important, significant and comfortable. Very often these are subtle things, such as the Nokia boss who focused so well on our colleague Bruno when they had their first meeting, or the Royal Shakespeare Company director who runs courses that touch on how to speak and listen well at work. At the start of his workshops he deliberately dials down his skills as a communicator, so that he doesn't intimidate participants with an impossibly polished exemplar.

KEY MESSAGES

- Trust and risk go hand in hand. We have something to say, then we think about the consequences.

- People make risk/reward judgement calls when deciding to speak up or not. While the risks of speaking up are often clear, the rewards are very rarely as obvious.

- Risk is social – it often comes down to being included or excluded.

- We stay silent if we think consequences are unknowable or unmanageable, if we think there's no point to speaking up, that someone else will if we don't, or if we think it might result in more work.

- Risk is a function of how powerful or powerless people feel they are. When power distance increases, so does risk.

- We underestimate how scary we are to others.

- Creating safety is in the gift of the more powerful.

- Social and organisational culture influences whether it's okay to challenge authority.

- Workplace forums and processes sometimes ignore the impact of power difference and therefore underestimate perceptions of risk.

If you do only one thing now, consider one person who you'd like to hear from that probably finds you scary. Next time you meet them, figure out how to reduce the power difference between you.

NOTES

1. https://www.theguardian.com/commentisfree/2017/dec/01/
    speaking-up-against-sexual-harassment-is-stilltoo-risky-for-most-
    women
2. https://www.newstatesman.com/politics/uk/2016/11/my-visor-
    down-against-night-i-unhooked-my-safetytether
3. https://www.theguardian.com/commentisfree/2008/nov/18/
    response-credit-crisis-economy-response
4. For more on this sort of double-bind see: Kegan, R. and Lahey,
    L. (2016) '*How the Way We Talk Can Change the Way We Work*'.
    Harvard Business Review Press.
5. https://www.xero.com/blog/2015/10/pressure-is-a-privilege-lessons-
    on-leadership-from-the-allblacks/
6. https://news.nationalgeographic.com/news/2013/07/130709-
    asiana-flight-214-crash-korean-airlinesculture-outliers/
7. https://hbr.org/2014/05/navigating-the-cultural-minefield
8. https://www.theguardian.com/business/2018/apr/20/
    barclays-ceo-jes-staley-facing-fine-overwhistleblower-incident
9. www.talkingmats.com
10. www.blobtree.com

CHAPTER 4

UNDERSTANDING: NAVIGATING THE UNWRITTEN RULES OF POLITICS AND POWER

To speak up and listen up effectively, you have to understand the political environment around you. Learning how to read the unwritten rules of the game is vital for your success and your career.

This is about deciphering politics and being able to spot the difference between the official and unofficial rulebook. It is about navigating the ways of the classroom – where there's a clear authority figure to enforce order and structure – and the playground, where things are messier and less open to official sanction.

You will learn:

- how to gauge and understand the political environment and what it might mean for speaking up and listening up

- how politics affects who you listen to, what you get to hear and what you don't

- when you are at most risk of misunderstanding politics and therefore when you are likely to speak up or listen up poorly

- *what the political environment is like in your team, department or organisation*
- *what helps you to speak up and listen up more effectively in your political environment.*

Politics can be thought of as the rules of the game through which power gets exercised and decisions get made. These unwritten rules can be candidly and correctly reflected in the published ways of working and the cultural values that are on display in the reception area. Or they can be in complete opposition to them.

What we choose to say and hear in our workplace takes place in a political context of competing agendas – and we are always part of someone's agenda. Speaking up and listening up are therefore always political acts in that they are never neutral. Someone or some group always stands to gain, or lose, when something gets said that challenges or reinforces the status quo.

Although politics is everywhere, present whenever there are people negotiating ideas or recommending actions, we often use the words 'office politics' in a derogatory fashion. It's taken to denote the misuse of power and influence to further individual priorities, usually with negative consequences for others.

Sometimes politics can be self-serving and murky. However, it can also be inspirational, bringing groups together to achieve amazing things. Engaging in politics is unavoidable and does not have to entail selling your soul.

SPEAKING UP IN A POLITICAL WORKPLACE

In order to influence what gets done and how you get heard at work you need to understand the political environment you are speaking into. Understanding your political environment means:

- knowing who has what type of power and influence in your organisation
- being able to assess what their agenda and priorities are.

Over half of the respondents who have completed our diagnostic say that they find it difficult to assess the priorities and agendas of those with power and influence.

MO

Mo, a rising star in a global technology firm we interviewed, attended his first all-company meeting in Atlanta, Georgia. It was plain to him that the power in the company rested with the movers and shakers in North America. When the time came for people to nominate who they wanted as their line manager in the year ahead, Mo asked for Tony, the head of the Chicago office. He chose to ignore Shikha, the woman who'd recruited him into the London operation. He'd had a really good conversation with Tony and they'd clicked. Little did he know that Shikha had been Tony's protégé for many years and they were very good friends. They always kept an eye open for each other's back and interests.

Shikha was less than impressed by what she saw as Mo's attempt to sideline her and discount her ambition to build up the London team (an ambition she and Tony shared). His next promotion was delayed a year and he was eating humble pie (apologising and trying to make amends) for a good while longer.

WHO HAS THE POWER?

Identifying who has power and influence can be extremely obvious in some cases, but it is always worth pausing and questioning our first assumptions. Although we often use the hierarchical structure as a proxy, you can probably point to individuals in your workplace who are senior, but not particularly influential, or conversely, who are junior but wield considerable influence.

We also can't restrict our assessment to individuals. It is vital to assess the overall political lay of the land: how political power is organised through relationships. This tells you whether, for example, powerful others act together in unison or whether they tend to oppose one another.

We believe it is more useful to see our organisations as systems or webs of political influence rather than hierarchical pyramids. Job titles are one thing but personality and social links (which might stretch outside the organisation) count for a lot. Megan remembers, with some humour, how long it took her to realise that two of the board members she was working closely with were married. Many decisions were as likely to be made around the dining room table in the evening as they were in the formal meetings Megan attended.

An alternative to viewing power as being equivalent to the latest organisational structure is to use metaphor. The family is one starting point, drawing as it does on everyone's first experience of power and authority in action, but this can be problematic as it can evoke strongly negative as well as positive emotional responses. John prefers to work with metaphors that come from fictional stories, films and TV to unhook people from an overly rationalistic take on human life, allowing them to explore power with more of an emotional (but not too personal) edge.

Think about your workplace and a situation you want to get talked about in public. Who are the characters that occupy different roles? What play, film or tv series best describes how decisions get made around you?

- Are you in *Game of Thrones*? Do people come and go with bloody haste? Or are you in a comfortable soap opera where everyone comes together at the end of the day?

- What about the Simpsons? Is there a somewhat clumsy but well-meaning person at the top? Who is the more mischievous Bart, forever disrespecting authority, the moral Lisa or the grounded Marge?

- Are you in King Lear or Hamlet? Do you have a retiring leader who wishes to retain some power and is easily flattered by those who would take over his or her divided kingdom?

- Are you in Cinderella? Who's the downtrodden one, who's expected to save the day and who's conspiring against who?

POWER'S NOT A THING

Once we have our view of our political web and metaphor, we then need to hold it lightly. In other words, we need to be aware that what we have is not 'right' or in any way objective.

Questions, such as who has power, how do you spot it and how is it structured, assume power is a thing and that we can all agree who has it and who hasn't. They also assume that the question 'power to do what?' doesn't affect our assessment. Someone who is powerful in day-to-day operations may suddenly appear less so when the new CEO brings in a change agenda.

Perceptions of power are just that – perceptions. Therefore, even while there may be broad agreement on the power structure in an organisation, different people will perceive and experience it differently. Barry Oshry has done compelling work around how different the world looks and feels depending on whether you are at the top, middle or bottom of an organisation.[1] And context matters. A sudden change in the company's fortune or a move from focusing on operations to innovation can markedly alter our view of who holds power and why.

When we interact with others, as well as holding our overall view on the other person's status in the system, we are navigating perceptions of our *relative* power and status. Accordingly, moment by moment we make choices on what we say and whether and how we listen.

Cast your mind back to when we described how Megan met her new CEO for the first time. Her perception of power going into that meeting had been rather static and one-dimensional: he had power because he was at the top of the hierarchy. Her understanding though of relative power shifted and changed as the conversation progressed. For example, she realised that he regarded her as relatively powerful because she was a leadership expert and that shifted her understanding of the political environment.

We can say therefore that power is relative, contextual, dynamic and very much subjective, existing at a macro, systemic level and within moment-by-moment interactions and relationships. Although we might be tempted to simplify power into who has it, who doesn't and how much we have, doing so limits our ability to skilfully understand politics and with that, speak up effectively.

WHAT'S ON THEIR AGENDA?

Figuring out who has power is one thing, but political awareness requires you also to ascertain what priorities and agenda powerful others hold. If you have a blind spot here, then you risk speaking up in a less than effective way.

MARY

Mary has a learning and development brief and has been tasked with introducing the executive teams of all units to the benefits of 'systems thinking'. She's a genuine believer in its potential and takes every opportunity to act as an advocate. She recently met with the CFO of one unit, who listened politely to her for ten minutes before butting in with words to the effect of: 'I have a $60m deficit I have to put right in the next six months. How can this help me? Because if I don't fix that $60m hole, there is no future.' Mary continued for a few minutes, then realised that she had not thought through how she could help with the fire-fighting exercise which was all the CFO could focus on.

Although she spoke up, she was not and could not be heard.

Determining other people's priorities in order to more effectively speak up to them requires you to be able to step into their shoes (and out of yours) and then rigorously check the assumptions you have made. Here's a guide:

- **Stop what you're doing and take a quiet moment:** Close your eyes perhaps and imagine what it is like to be the person you are wanting to speak up to. What might keep them awake at night? What do they gain satisfaction from achieving? What motivates them? How might they want to be perceived by others? What *matters* to them?

- **Ask others:** Don't just ask those people that come from the same team as you or who see the world in very similar ways. If you find the person in question difficult, don't just ask someone who also finds them difficult – ask someone who seems to interact very well with them. The way you phrase your request is important. You can explain that you want to raise something and that you know the person you're speaking with is effective at doing this (flattery helps). You could ask: 'What's on 'x's' mind?', 'How do they like to hear ideas?' or 'What is the most effective way to raise issues or challenges?'

- **Ask them:** But don't assume that what the person says are their priorities are definitely their priorities. The published message might be that they are interested in creativity and innovation, but in reality quarterly figures may just seem more of a priority at the moment. Try asking them, 'What objectives are you working to?', 'What do you think is most challenging right now and why?' or 'What is your boss or the board most focused on? What are they pressing you for?'

- **Speak up with their priorities in mind:** Even if you can't align what you have to say with something that the other person wants or would gain from, show that you have at least considered them.

LISTENING UP IN A POLITICAL WORKPLACE

Skilfully accounting for politics when you *listen* up requires you to:

- judge when people are telling you what they think you want to hear
- know when people are telling you something they want you to pass on to influential others.

The COO in the major international bank reflected on how he thought he was being helpful when touring the trading desks and making suggestions.

He was told that these suggestions were really valuable, but later he realised that in some cases people felt compelled to work on them even though they knew they were no good.

When John worked with a Danish executive team recently he was told by a manager: 'We're a team until there's a shit storm. Then you're on your own.' The person who told John this knew that the company's executives could not hear that from her – not after they'd spent the last two years extolling what a united and collective team they were. She knew however much the execs advocated the need not to blame the messenger, in practice they probably would. But they could hear it from John. So that's the route she took.

Let's look at the two aspects of listening up we identified at the start of this section in more detail.

YOUR JOKES SEEM TO BE GETTING FUNNIER

As you get more powerful, your jokes get funnier as the saying goes. In other words, the more powerful we are the more people around us might want to please us. As well as laughing at our jokes (even if they are not at all funny), others may settle into a habit of telling or showing us what they think we want to hear.

Do you notice that:

- You rarely get challenged – mostly people agree with you.
- You get complimented on your ideas – a lot.
- You have to really work hard to get others to tell you alternative perspectives.
- The picture you get given by others is unusually positive.
- People agree with your agenda for change – and then things stay as they are.

Alan Mulally, former president of Ford Motor Company, explained how, in the year when he joined the company, it was forecast to lose $17 billion. Yet in his first business plan review meeting, he was presented with charts from all over the global business that were 'green' – reporting that things were going well. He paused proceedings and said: 'Guys, we are going to lose $17 billion. Is there anything that's not going well here?'[2]

MEGAN AND THE ROYAL VISIT

Megan helped run a business simulation for a team as part of their leadership development programme. The team suddenly heard from head office that they were to be visited by a member of the British royal family as part of an official tour. The most extraordinary amount of preparation was then initiated and Megan was asked to help: 'At 11.04am this important member of the royal family is due to walk through our office and we need to be doing something interesting. Will you just come and run that closing bit on the leadership simulation with us again?'

'So, let me get this straight,' Megan said, 'you want me to simulate the leadership simulation at 11.04 tomorrow?' 'Exactly.'

It occurred to Megan at this point that the unsuspecting member of the royal family may well be none the wiser that what they were to witness at 11.04 was an entirely scripted and sanitised version of reality. And why would they? All their life they have visited people who have spent hours perfecting a version of truth for them to see.

You may not be a member of the royal family, but if you're in a position of authority you *are* scary and you are likely to be on the receiving end of a similar smoke screen where people are second-guessing what sort of experience you want or need to have and are often fearful of being judged poorly.

You'll need to be skilful in inviting them to speak up if you want to get to something other than the truth they think you want to hear.

IT'S NOT *YOU* THEY WANT TO TELL

Listening up in a political environment means we also need to determine why someone is telling us what they are. If we are influential, it is likely that some things we get to hear are told to us because others want us to pass something on to other influential persons.

SAMANTHA

Samantha is responsible for managing a stake in a major public company. Paul, who works for a rival investment company, also has responsibility for overseeing an investment in the same company. Samantha is getting

▶

increasingly concerned by what she is seeing going on in its board room and gives Paul a call, describing what she's seen. Paul is now in the loop and is motivated to act. He leads a robust conversation with the chair and CEO the next time he meets with them.

Whenever Samantha had tried to have such a conversation she'd been frozen out, but now she'd got what she wanted – a public debate about whether the executive team were fit for purpose. She had to pass on her insights to someone who was part of the old boys network to get her insights heard. She might not like it, but her age and gender ruled her out in this case.

In one family firm we explored, it was striking how there was one non-family member who was trusted by everyone in the family to be the one who could tell the son and heir what they believed he needed to know. And it was this outsider that the heir apparent was able to hear. The outsider knew that their role was to be a conduit to power, not to act as if they had power that only a family member could have.

THE SPEAK UP, LISTEN UP CULTURE AND THE GAMES PEOPLE PLAY

Whether speaking up or listening up, we need to spot the games that are being played around us and how we are wittingly or unwittingly engaging in them. In all workplaces there is a politically correct quality to organisational discourse. The game is around knowing what you're allowed and expected to talk about and what is frowned upon.

Through our research and backed up by a substantial body of academic texts and management literature, we have discovered that the following subjects are often regarded as safer and easier to talk about. Are they in your workplace? You need to know. It affects what you can say and what you listen to:

■ **Tangible things** that are measurable (key performance indicators, financial performance) rather than intangible aspects such as wellbeing and motivation. The latter can become more acceptable when it is defined in terms of KPIs or benchmarked statistically. A government minister gave one of our interviewees the instruction to 'Sweat the data until it gives me what I want'. Decisions were made at the top of government assuming the tangible data was 'correct'.

It may be a cliché, but the old saying still holds true, there are lies, damned lies and statistics.

- **Perspectives that suggest change is good and can be managed,** rather than perspectives that consider change as unpredictable and likely to have negative consequences for some groups.

An organisation we visited proudly displays as one of its core values that people need to be 'Positive about change'. The intention may be good but it de-legitimises and pushes into the shadows all doubts.

- **A budget that fits** with senior stakeholder priorities, but is unachievable rather than a budget that isn't great, but is realistic. Our financial COO called the budget process 'the organisation's biggest lie'.

A CEO of a hospital in the NHS we talked to signed his professional death warrant by being honest about what his hospital budget would be at the start of the year. Publicly funded health budgets are a 'big P' (i.e. governmental-level) political issue. He explained that within health the accepted tradition is that everyone says the budget is achievable right up until the last month of the year when everyone announces a deficit at more or less the same time. Aggressive pressure was brought to bear on him until he decided he'd had enough and resigned. A star CEO was parachuted in and promised to deliver to a new non-deficit budget. The year ended with the hospital delivering exactly to the original deficit budget.

- **Achievements that portray us as perfect** rather than mistakes that illustrate how we are imperfect.

John was creating a case study for a major global advisory firm a while back. He agreed to change geography and sector in order to leave the firm unidentifiable. However, because it was a case study about an internal project that had gone wrong the firm refused to allow it to be used either internally or externally. The firm did not want its clients or regulators to think it could ever be less than perfect. The politics of perfection mean that mistakes get silenced and learning is unlikely to happen.

- **Those who are more senior know best** rather than knowledge and expertise might be found throughout the organisation.

We spoke with Jamie who, in his twenties, is an expert in cyber security. He joined a large advisory firm where the partnership structure is attached to the idea that the partner is always the expert in front of the client. The expert partner, who Jamie reported to, started selling cyber security services that simply were not appropriate. So Jamie left and joined a specialist firm where his technical expertise is valued more highly than his hierarchical position.

- **We talk active collaboration** rather than admit we are apathetic or competitive.

  While working in an intellectual property (IP) role for a global professional services firm, John discovered a rivalry between the US and Germany offices. Neither office valued the IP that came out of the other. John found that locating new IP as coming out of the Netherlands office got round a lot of this rivalry.

  In the NHS, new systemic business models are being advocated which bring together health and social care. One of our interviewees, Mike, attends the board meetings of the various representatives of the constituent bodies. They say they take the central directive to collaborate seriously, but nothing ever happens. They are possibly wise to the idea that another initiative will arrive within a year, so if they talk this one out all will be fine.

Seeing the games is vital. Speaking up, counter to the games above, will be risky and we may need to tread carefully.

Listening up with *discernment* requires an ability to lift ourselves out of the game playing and take a more critical view on our conversations. If we don't, we risk believing naively and wholeheartedly what people say and taking it as truth.

WHEN YOU'RE MOST AT RISK OF MISREADING POLITICS

There are times when we are more at risk of misreading our workplace politics. At these times we need to be especially vigilant about how we speak up and listen up:

- **When you're new to an organisation:** Often when we join an organisation we are privileged to spot strange ways of working that those who have been there a while can no longer see. However, while we find our bearings and learn the 'language' it is especially easy for us to make faux pas.

  A direct and formidable American female executive joined a more traditional British organisation we were working with – and lasted only six months. Her difference was extremely valuable and needed, but she was unable to figure out the politics and temper her behaviour in a way that would invite others to listen to what she had to say. And frustratingly, the organisation did not have the openness to accommodate her.

- **When you get promoted:** People act differently towards us once we've become more senior – we are told different things and listened to in different ways. If we are used to being "one of the guys" this can come as a surprise, as it did to Francois, the newly promoted MD Megan was coaching, who noticed after his promotion had been communicated that his colleagues began to exit his office.

- **During a merger or acquisition:** When two cultures combine it is uncertain what the end-product will be. Who has status and authority is in flux and people vie for their reputation and a decent role in the new venture.

- **When there is upheaval at senior levels:** The entry of a new CEO or new directors can shake things up at the top. We are unsure as to who has what sort of power and influence and whether the old way will win through or a new order is about to begin.

- **When you're bought in for your difference:** Often a compliment but sometimes a poison chalice, we can be invited into a team because of our different perspective. Similar to the American executive above, an ex-investment banker was invited to join the executive team of a housing association we worked with in order to bring greater commercial and financial literacy into the team. He lasted three months as his difference was too much for the rest of the executive to cope with.

  This is a paradox of group dynamics[3] and how they shape what is said and heard. We are invited to join groups because of the different voice and insight we bring, but to stay in the group we have to give up that difference and talk and listen like everyone else.

HOW TO ASSESS YOUR WORKPLACE POLITICAL CULTURE

Political forces affect whose voice gets heard. If we don't know who has what power, are blind to our own influence in the system and can't see the games that are being played, then we are unlikely to speak or listen up effectively. Our agenda gets buried by the agendas of others.

We've discussed how you can bring power into view. Now we will ask you to reflect on the political culture you face at work. Culture defines habits of speaking up and listening up. Knowing the culture you work in will highlight different opportunities and traps for speaking truth to power.

The truth–power framework has been developed from analysing our interviews, ethnographic studies and collaborative inquiries. It assesses workplace culture along two dimensions:

1. **How power is used:** Whether it is used by the more powerful in order to exert their own view and control outcomes (power *over*), or whether it is used in order to enable collective action, facilitating others to voice and act in the way they feel appropriate (power *with*).

2. **How truth is viewed:** Whether there is one truth which is ordained by those in power and is not to be questioned (*single* truth), or whether diverse truths are invited, considered and questioned openly (*multiple* truths).

If we illustrate these dimensions on a matrix, we arrive at four political cultures as shown in the figure below. Let's look at the implications of each of these in turn in relation to speaking up and listening up – and please note no culture will be a pure version of any one of these. As you read through the different cultures, think about what aspects are relevant to your workplace.

THE TRUTH–POWER FRAMEWORK

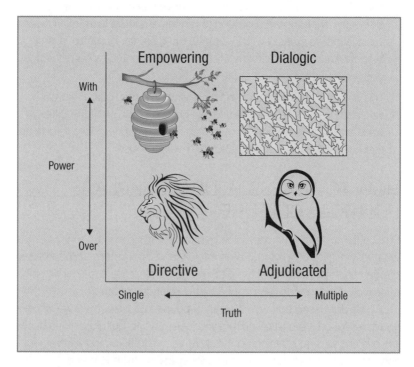

The directive 'lion' culture

A directive culture has a single all-powerful individual (or group of individuals) who sets the vision, strategy and agenda and they expect others to follow rather than question it. There is a single truth – a right path, and power is used to exert control over others' actions and make that truth happen.

Speaking up against this single truth needs to be approached with caution. It is more effective if you have developed personal trust with the person or people in power and know the specific circumstances in which they will listen.

The deputy chair of one of the world's largest advertising companies told us that he quickly learnt not to challenge the chair in a group setting, but if he waited until they were both alone, sitting down with a glass of wine in the evening at a hotel on their business travels, then the chair would listen to him.

Speaking up in a directive culture requires knowing the ways to influence the person in charge.

Listening up requires you to see the power you hold if you're the lion. You are likely to hear what people think you want to hear. You need to ask yourself what consequences you face if you don't invite alternative perspectives in. Even if you are not willing to hand over the reins, ask yourself what aspects you *do* want to hear challenge on. Consider how you will invite those challenges, given that it is unlikely employees will offer their perspectives willingly.

The directive culture is often viewed as outdated but is nevertheless still common. It can be a stifling and intimidating place to work if the person in charge is domineering and unapproachable. Then compliance is the only way to survive. However, it can be exciting and energising if they are inspirational and charismatic or safe and secure if they are paternalistic.

Think about your workplace through the lens of this culture:

1. Is there one individual or group whose views dominate what gets talked about and what gets heard?
2. Who is successful in influencing this individual or group?
3. How can *you* be more successful in influencing this individual or group?
4. And if you're the one who dominates, how do you hear from more than the usual suspects?

The empowering 'queen bee' culture

In the empowering culture there is a clearly identifiable, dominant leader who is akin to the 'queen bee'. As in nature, the worker bees are there to serve the needs of the queen, but, unlike in the directive culture, are given the power to self-organise and work together in order to make the hive a success.

A leadership team Megan worked with from a retail organisation had taken themselves off on a leadership retreat and returned with the organisational strategy. This was a fait accompli – a single truth – and included the requirement for a rather arbitrary 20% ROI from each department. This target was farmed out to the departments who were given carte blanche to do what they needed to as long as they hit the target. The leadership team used their power to take out roadblocks that were getting in the way of delivery and to provide the necessary resources.

Depending on the consequences at stake if you don't hit targets, the empowering culture can feel safe in that there is certainty about direction and rewarding in that there is still enough manoeuvrability to make decisions. But as with the example of the retailer above, an empowering culture can feel frustrating as our power to influence the overall strategic direction is limited.

Speaking up in this culture requires us to make sure we have our 'fighter cover' firmly in place. This means spending time clarifying what the target is, playing back what has been said and making sure we have a really clear understanding of exactly what we are being asked to achieve. This then allows us to figure out the boundaries of where we have scope to challenge without risk and where we don't.

Listening up means that, as leaders, we need to acknowledge what aspects of what we have said is up for discussion and what isn't. We need to absent ourselves from some conversations in order to enable others to get on with things but need to be available to listen out for ways in which we can clear the path. We need to be prepared to accept points of view on *how* things should be done when they differ with our own. We also need to exercise patience and empathy if we are asking others to step up and deliver but we encounter resistance. If previous regimes have limited the power that is handed down the hierarchy then it is no surprise there is reticence now in taking the initiative. If you have threatened others explicitly or implicitly with the consequences of underachievement don't be surprised if they keep problems to themselves until it's too late.

Think about your workplace through the lens of this culture:

1. Is there one group or individual whose views dominate the setting of direction?
2. Are you left free to work out how best to achieve your goals?
3. What do you do when you can see that the goal and direction look impossible or wrong?
4. How can you be more successful in influencing the direction-setting conversation?
5. And if you're the one who sets the goals, are you hearing the views that you need to hear in order to do that well?

The adjudicated 'owl' culture

In the adjudicated culture multiple perspectives are expected and invited, then the wise owl exerts their power over proceedings in order to judge which ideas will get actioned. Their decision, a bit like in a courtroom, is considered final.

When the adjudicated culture is working effectively, there is rigorous debate amongst opposing perspectives enabling a richer understanding of context prior to decisions being made. When it works poorly we find ourselves pitched against our colleagues and there can be an explosion in politicking as we try our best to influence the decision-maker that our idea is the best one.

PRIYA

Priya, an HR director Megan was working with realised she had inadvertently created an adjudicated culture. In-fighting between her reports meant that rather than sorting out their differences themselves, she was being dragged into playground politics. Individuals were increasingly requesting one-to-ones with her to sell their ideas and condemn the ideas of others. Gradually Priya found herself spending more and more time stepping in to sort things out and make decisions about who was right. The more she did this, the more her team became reliant on her views and their capacity to collaborate vanished.

Speaking up in an adjudicated culture requires us to know how to present a compelling argument and be savvy enough to be aware of alternative views. We also need to be wise enough to speak up in a way that avoids petty competition developing. However, although it is often sensible to aim for a win–win and avoid alienating colleagues, sometimes there will be battles to be fought. We need therefore to feel comfortable with conflict.

When decisions go against us, we need to be able to speak up gracefully in support of the agreed strategy. We need to be able to lose well. *And* we need to be able to win well. When things go in our favour we need to speak up in a way that brings in our losing colleagues who have been pursuing alternative agendas.

Listening up in an adjudicated culture requires us to know when to invite others to speak up and when to silence them and say: 'You need to sort this out with the other person – and tell me the outcome.' We need to be able to facilitate the expression of opposing views and encourage a focus on the shared outcome while avoiding favouritism. We then must be capable of listening to the losing side once we've made a decision. We need to help them through their frustration, while knowing when to draw that to an end in order to get on with things.

Think about your workplace through the lens of this culture:

1. Do you spend a lot of time competing with other groups internally?
2. Do you spend a lot of time lobbying a clear group of decision-makers so that your area will win?
3. How can you be more successful in influencing this group?
4. What steps could you take to create more of a win–win culture?
5. And if you're the one who adjudicates, how do you encourage people to collaborate as well as compete?

The dialogic 'starling' culture

Although the other cultures have a relatively clear power structure in place, the dialogic culture is more tricky to fathom, as hierarchical power is limited and there may be no obvious chain-of-command. Typically, power is used to bring people together, share views and make decisions. Once people are together there are minimal rules, allowing the group to organise and reorganise themselves in ways that works for them.

This is akin to the way that starlings operate. The flock congregates into murmurations (large coordinated groups) and then constantly orders and re-orders itself during the course of its flight.

It can feel tremendously engaging and fulfilling as we feel our opinion is heard and we have power to influence the decisions that are made. We can experience this organisational culture as agile, creative and responsive to external challenges and opportunities. Our colleague Anthony's work on the strategy for the Kingdom of Uganda worked with a well-established dialogic culture where all groups are invited to speak and listen together.

On the other hand though, it can feel frustratingly unwieldy and develop into a talking-shop where there are painful rituals around listening to every view. We find ourselves avoiding exerting power in a way that could conceivably be viewed as anything other than entirely egalitarian.

Speaking up effectively in a dialogic culture means showing clear respect to other viewpoints and relishing difference. It requires us to own what we say, but be open to what others say because we understand there is no right or single answer. It means we take care not to dominate and speak over others (particularly if we are perceived as powerful). We also have to be able to skilfully speak up in order to finalise a decision and take action in a way which is not perceived as controlling.

Similarly, listening up means skilful inquiry to help and facilitate respectful sharing of different views. We need to know when the time for listening is at an end and a decision must be made. In this way, more than in the other cultures, speaking up and listening up go very much hand in hand. We find ourselves switching and moving between advocacy and inquiry multiple times.

Think about your workplace through the lens of this culture:

1. Are senior leaders more interested in hearing from people rather than talking at them?

2. Are decisions reached through a process of genuine and extensive participation?

3. Do you spend a lot of time talking things through so everyone is given the opportunity to make sense for themselves about what needs to happen and why?

4. Are people able to get hold of the information they need to make an informed contribution to conversations?

5. How can you be more successful in influencing these conversations?

NAVIGATING YOUR POLITICAL ENVIRONMENT

Many of our interviewees recommend we assess and reflect upon our political environment in order to speak up and listen up more effectively. We've talked through some things that help you do this:

- Metaphors for mapping power (for example movies and fictional stories).
- Examples of the games people play.
- A process for stepping into someone else's shoes.
- The truth–power cultural framework.

Other advice includes:

- **Observe role-models:** These are people who come across as politically savvy (but not disingenuous). What is it that they do that enables them to speak and listen up well? Which of these things, which might work for you, could you experiment with?
- **Name the elephants:** Politics, in its treacherous sense, thrives on secrecy. The rules of the game are unwritten and often not talked about. However, destructive rules can lose their potency if made explicit.

  Megan recalls working with a large group from the medical profession. The group contained people with a myriad of titles such as dames, lords, sirs, consultants, doctors and students. It was tremendously hierarchical; the pecking order created numerous issues and yet the conversation was around collaboration and inclusion. Carefully using her British sarcasm to best effect, Megan began to explain how the labels we give ourselves and others can silence and exclude: 'But of course, we all know that here that isn't a problem at all is it?' she said. Met, fortunately, with much humour, this comment opened up a rich conversation about the medical profession and the forms of privilege and entitlement that can defeat its aims to provide the best medical care to patients.

- **Be socially astute in order to be politically savvy:** This means being able to see how others see you, or 'other awareness'. How we see ourselves is not necessarily how others see us and this can be a significant surprise. We may need the help of a coach or a mentor to point out to us how our position, behaviour and network influences how others perceive our political power.

- **Develop the capacity to be critical:** This is not in the sense of criticising but in the sense of critiquing. This is invaluable in a political environment. We need to be able to question ourselves. Why am I saying this in this way to this person? Am I proud of my intentions here and the way I am choosing to behave? We also need to be able to question what we hear and see as truth as in 'If there was a reason I am being told this what would it be?'

More than anything, navigating your political environment is best done in the company of others. Having allies and people who have your back creates the social safety net that helps keep anxiety at bay. Think about who you have now in your network, and who you need to have, so you can continue to develop your skill in speaking up and listening up.

KEY MESSAGES

- Your workplace is political – you either play politics or get played.
- Your workplace will have rules of the game, its own unique political culture which shapes what is readily said and heard.
- Speaking up well, politically, requires you to know who has what type of power and influence. Then you need to be able to assess what their agenda and priorities are.
- Listening up well in a political environment requires you to judge when people are telling you what they think you want to hear. You also need to spot when people are telling you something they want you to pass on to influential others.
- There are likely to be unwritten rules in your workplace about what is okay to talk about (or listen to) and what isn't.
- There are times when you are most at risk of misreading politics, for example, when you are new or during structural changes.
- The truth–power framework describes four political cultures: directive, empowering, adjudicated and dialogic. It can help you to examine the implications on speaking up and listening up in your organisation.

If you only do one thing now, offer to be a useful ally to someone you can see is being silenced by politics.

NOTES

1. Oshry, Barry (2007) *Seeing Systems,* by Barry Oshry 2007, Berrett-Koehler Publishers.
2. https://www.youtube.com/watch?v=Zlwz1KlKXP4&t=1738s
3. Smith, Kenwyn K. and Berg, David, N. (1987) In *Human Relations,* October, 40 (10), 633–657.

CHAPTER 5

TITLES: HOW THEY GIVE AND TAKE AUTHORITY

We all go through life wearing titles. Some we choose for ourselves, some come with the job we do or the station we are at in life, and some are put on us by others. In this chapter, you will examine why you cannot help but apply titles, labels and categories to yourself and to others. You will discover how that process fundamentally affects whether you feel you have the status and authority to speak up and whether you consider others worthy of being listened to.

As human beings, we dole out titles and labels, such as CEO, woman, Asian, consultant, cashier, introvert and elderly, all the time. They convey differing levels of status and authority, depending on the context within which we find ourselves. These perceptions of status and authority then greatly affect whether we speak up and to whom we listen.

You will learn:

■ why and how you inevitably attach titles to yourself and to others, whether you are aware of doing so or not

- *how context, such as culture, history and professional discipline, affects the meaning – and the consequences – of these labels and titles*

- *how titles can be useful because of how they help us know which tribe others belong to and how they can best be engaged with*

- *which titles you attach to yourself and to others and how they affect how you speak up and are spoken to*

- *how the titles you attach to yourself and to others affect who you listen to*

- *why owning the labels we put on others, and others put on us, can be so difficult as they reveal prejudices and assumptions about who and what counts in the world.*

It is likely that you will learn that you unconsciously judge others unfairly or overly positively because of aspects of how they look or sound.

Just because we don't want to be biased against certain others – we vehemently oppose discrimination and want to engage with people on their merits – does *not* mean that we see others fairly and equally. Our unconscious mind sees to that. The sooner we realise this, the sooner we can engage in countering the often negative fallout from what is an inevitable process. And the sooner we can improve how we speak up and listen up.

Finding a way to talk about and own titles and their associated judgements is an important step in creating a real (rather than pretend) speak-up culture.

TITLES, TITLES AND MORE TITLES

If we stop and think for a moment, we begin to realise exactly how many titles, labels and categories we apply in our day-to-day interactions.

Imagine you are sitting on the train and you look around the carriage. It is likely that you will quickly label each person in at least five different ways within a fraction of a second according to their gender, age, race, weight and height. It is also quite possible that on top of these categorisations you will be able to add occupation, social class and religion, depending on what the person is wearing. It is quite extraordinary how quickly this process happens – and that we are able to settle on an understanding about strangers from such snapshot data.[1]

If we join a workplace team for its first meeting, we not only categorise according to the aspects above, but we also quickly add to our complex, rich picture of each team member by including titles such as sales, techie, director, junior, new or experienced. Many teams make indiscriminate use of the Myers-Briggs Type Indicator (MBTI), or other psychometrics, and we can be quick to fix someone with a single label or title. For example, if they're loud and talkative the first time we meet them we may label them as being an extrovert (which isn't the correct definition). We overlook that they may have been nervous and anxious on that first meeting and that they are actually someone who usually needs inviting to speak.

And of course, as we are labelling others, they are busy applying titles and labels to *us.*

Occasionally, we have some awareness that this is going on. We might try to influence this process. For example, we credentialise – pick out key words and titles that we think might make a good impression.

Sue, a nurse who had attended a conference talk Megan had given, told her about a meeting she had attended where a new member of the team had used no less than eight titles to introduce himself, covering his academic, professional and organisational standing. No doubt, he felt that this would raise his profile and status in the group. Perhaps it did for some but Sue just seemed to find it amusing.

We might decide to use formal job titles, name-drop past organisations we have worked with, indicate that we have travelled widely and casually refer to important people we are friends with.

Although such credentialising might be a conscious choice, much of the labelling we do is *unconscious.* This process has the advantage of enabling us to form opinions quickly, but the consequences can be extreme when it turns into stereotyping – fixing set characteristics to a group that may or may not reflect reality.

So why do we do it?

SAFETY IN THE SAME NUMBERS

The most common explanation of why we apply titles and labels in a fraction of a second is an evolutionary one. Our ancestors lived in small homogenous communities, surrounded by constant threat from other communities. It became a matter of survival to be able to see another person and quickly identify them as one of us or one of them. We learnt to stay away from people who were different to us.

However, doing that is precisely what we now realise we *shouldn't* do in the workplace. Diversity is linked positively to results, innovation, meeting the customer's needs, challenging ways of working which are outdated and making robust decisions. Additionally of course, in many places discriminating based on gender, age, sexual orientation or ethnicity is illegal. It is not therefore surprising that so many workplaces now strongly advocate diversity and inclusion.

But just because we *shouldn't* or *don't want to* discriminate doesn't mean we *don't*. Explicitly exploring how we discriminate in the workplace might well be viewed by many as a legal minefield, as it would mean admitting to practices that are not meant to go on. Digging into these taken-for-granted assumptions about what we actually do at work (rather than what we espouse) would also require slowing down to notice what we usually speed past. Slowing down to reflect is not a popular activity in a working world. There is a largely unquestioned belief in the importance of speed, even if that speed has many of the qualities of the fridge magnet that reads 'Drink coffee – and do more stupid things faster'.

I DON'T DISCRIMINATE

We worked with the staff from a retirement community who wanted to improve the way they respected and related with one another. When it came to a discussion on the titles and labels that they were applying to each other they were offended and said that of course they weren't biased, and how could they be when it was illegal.

In our survey, we ask respondents how often social bias in relation to gender, age, job title and race affects the way they listen to others. How would you respond to this question? As we mentioned, one respondent found the mere fact of being asked this question offensive.

Does a person's gender affect the way you listen? If you think it does, how often? Rarely? Sometimes? Often? And what about their age? Surely, their job title might influence how you judge them and therefore how you listen?

Admitting to the existence of certain biases can be difficult, as well as provocative. On average we found a staggering 91% of respondents are convinced that gender rarely or never affects the way they listen. The statistic is similar with race.

Our respondents are more willing to admit job title and age might affect how they listen, but even then most think they don't. 62% and 78% respectively think that it rarely or never affects their listening.

Perhaps our respondents are unlike any other human beings in their capacity to neutralise judgement. Alternatively, more likely, they genuinely (but wrongly) believe that they are in control of their judgement. Or, perhaps, similar to the staff at the retirement community, they simply do not want to admit (even in an anonymous survey) that they might discriminate based on social bias.

MARVIN

Megan recently ran the survey with a large pharmaceutical organisation. Apparently, 100% of the survey respondents in this organisation believed that race did not affect the way they listened to others. When Megan showed the results on the screen, Marvin, the one black manager in the audience at this point, put his head in his hands. 'Let me give you a different perspective on that," he said, and proceeded to explain the subtle but corrosive prejudice he had become accustomed to at work.

We like to think of ourselves as ethically and morally upstanding. We rely on the belief that we are masters of our own minds and capable of objectivity. But as Harvard University researcher Mahzarin Banaji simply states, in this regard 'more than two decades of research confirms that, in reality, most of us fall woefully short of our inflated self-perception'.[2] Most psychologists now agree that much of human judgement and decision-making is made without conscious thought.

BUT I ADVOCATE EQUAL RIGHTS

You may have heard of the IAT, the Implicit Association Test, developed by Banaji and Greenwald.[3] The IAT examines *implicit* attitudes and beliefs that people are either unwilling or unable to report. It measures association between categories and in particular whether those categories are linked via shared goodness or badness, or in more psychological terms, positive or negative valence.

In their book *Blind Spot,* they tell this story:

> *'In Jan 2005, Washington Post reporter Shankar Vedantam wrote a story about our research. One of his interviewees, a gay activist, had predictably expressed strong pro-gay attitudes during the interview. Vedantam then invited her to take an IAT to measure her automatic preference for gay versus straight groups. The activist was stunned by the result. The IAT revealed that her own mind contained stronger gay=bad associations than gay=good associations. One mind, two opposing preferences – one the product of her mind's reflective thinking, the other of the same mind's automatic associations.'[4]*

We can believe one thing with all our heart (and reflective mind), but we cannot escape the experiences that our minds have been subject to all our lives. The jokes, stories, news headlines, images, fairy tales, movies, day-to-day language and celebrities we admire persistently drip-feed messages to us. Many of us have been prompted again and again to develop automatic associations that connect things such as black with aggression, male with career, female with family, Asians with being good at maths, African Americans with success in sport and being overweight with lower intelligence. We don't notice the subtle message wrapped up in our use of terms such as 'stay-at-home dad' or 'working mum' (when the converse – 'stay-at-home mum' and 'working dad' are simply not phrases in our repertoire).

You are unlikely to be fully aware of the titles and labels you are applying to your work colleagues, let alone whether you are linking those titles and labels inextricably with positive or negative assumptions.

And therefore it is likely, along with the vast majority of people we have worked with, that you have a blind spot around how this process of categorisation affects whether you speak up and who you listen to.

DO *YOU* HAVE ADVANTAGE BLINDNESS?

The titles we give ourselves and others convey differing levels of status and authority *depending* on the context we are in.

Our colleague, Ben Fuchs, writes of a story[5] told to him by the retired CEO of a large British corporation. This CEO took part in an activity designed to highlight what titles and labels gave career advantage in their organisation. For example, they listed nationality, gender, education (especially which universities), age and marital status.

> 1. What labels count in your workplace?
> 2. What would your list look like?

The facilitator lined the group up shoulder to shoulder and went through the list of labels instructing them to take one step forward for each one that they 'owned' that gave them an advantage. Ben recalls that 'at the end the CEO was way out in front of the rest of the group, having taken a step forward on each and every point of the list'.

> 1. Which of the labels that count in your workplace apply to you?
> 2. How many steps forward would you take relative to others?

How did this experience of his advantage make this CEO feel? Ben quotes the CEO as saying: 'I had always thought my success was down to a lot of hard work and some innate talents. But I realised on that day that I also had every advantage to help me get to the top.'

MEGAN

As an example of the impact of owning the wrong titles, Megan recalls working as a management consultant in her twenties. She was frequently asked to undertake analysis and then present it at board meetings for the consultancy's clients. In a performance review one year her manager said to her: 'The problem is Megan, when you come into the board room, the client labels you as young and woman.' She knew that sometimes she was even given the title of 'girl'. Her manager was not admonishing Megan for something she could do nothing about, but his point was there was an inconvenient truth around her age and gender that meant that she needed to work hard to be taken seriously. This matched with Megan's experience – and she spent a good few years experimenting with combinations of glasses and scarfs to make herself appear older (something that is not so necessary any more).

Now there may be some contexts where the titles 'young' and 'woman' convey status and authority. We can't, unfortunately, think of many, but the point here is that titles get their meaning depending on context. 'Director' in one organisation might convey significant power and authority. They might be seen to be the one with the final say or someone who should not be challenged. In another, less hierarchical organisation the title might hold very little sway. Young in one organisation might convey inexperience and low status. But in a technology start-up, young might convey more savviness and knowhow.

Although we are often aware if we possess the wrong labels, it can be much harder to see if we possess the right ones. If we are already part of the 'in-group' majority, we are less likely to see the challenges of those in the 'out-group' minority. Our colleague, Ben, coined this 'advantage blindness'.[6]

BUT TITLES CAN BE VERY USEFUL

So far we have spoken of titles and our habit of putting them on people as an inevitable and largely negative process. But this habit of wearing titles can be very useful both to ourselves and to others.

Titles can let people know where we're coming from, what work tribe we belong to and so what to expect from us. If we refer back to the man with eight titles, he may have been displaying his ego and he may have been revealing as much as possible about the context and world that he inhabited so that people could engage well with him.

John has been shadowing a major research study into mental health and justice.[7] It brings together people from the physical science tradition of neuroscience, and other 'truth disciplines' such as anthropology, sociology and the law. It also includes the perspectives of health practitioners working with people with mental health issues, as well as people living with conditions. Part of the collaborative process has been to be explicit about the titles people wear as they take part in the work so that they can notice when they are bumping up against very different assumptions about what counts as evidence and truth.

The same words mean very different things when said by people wearing different titles.

In following the work of a senior barrister in court, John was taken by surprise when this erudite and sophisticated man directly addressed the Judge and said that what was being proposed 'wasn't fair'. It sounded almost childish as a complaint to John's ear. Afterwards the barrister explained that in a legal context, to make a claim that something wasn't fair was to make a very serious point and not one to be used lightly. Justice must both be fair and be seen to be fair.

If we don't know the titles someone has it can be very hard to make sense of why they say what they say.

PUTTING ON AND PUTTING ASIDE OUR TITLES

ROWAN WILLIAMS

When Megan interviewed Rowan Williams, Archbishop of Canterbury between 2002 and 2012, she found him to be very much as his public persona suggests. He wears his titles lightly and seems to be free of much of the egoism that goes with people who hold, or have held, high office. One parish priest John spoke with subsequently told of how Rowan came to a service in his suburban London parish, travelling by tube, bringing his own sandwiches and engaging with whole-hearted attention with the lives of the members of the congregation as they talked after the service.

▶

Yet in his interview, Rowan Williams told the story of the time when he had to demonstrate the Church of England's displeasure with approaches being made to certain members of its clergy by the Church of Rome. The cardinal (a senior representative of the Pope), was summoned to Lambeth Palace and Rowan Williams (then Archbishop) wore all his trappings of office and met the cardinal in the most ancient and impressive settings available in the palace. His intention was to communicate that he was speaking with the full authority of his title and of the history that represented and that the issue they were going to discuss was serious and of the utmost importance.

On a more day-to-day level, the CEO of a global youth charity spoke of her experience of engaging with a junior member of staff. In an informal setting, this member of staff, who was a friend, complained of experiencing discrimination. The CEO then spoke as a friend and suggested some informal advice on what might be a useful next step for them. She also said that if that didn't work and this person still felt discriminated against, or even didn't feel the informal suggestion was appropriate, then she would have to respond to it with her 'CEO hat' on. That response would have to reflect her formal position and the need to initiate the approved formal process. What she was trying to do was negotiate between the title of friend and confidante and the positional title of CEO – and all the responsibilities of office that came with that title.

Within military settings there are formal protocols when people name that they are setting aside their badges of rank and conversations are taking place without the presence of those titles. At the end of the conversation, badges of rank are put back on and the formal authority and chain of command is re-established. In one Asian bank, the CEO confirmed the anecdotal story that formally approved drinking sessions are the settings where titles are put to one side and anything can be said (and forgotten) the next day.

Do you find yourself navigating between on-the-record and off-the-record conversations in the workplace? To do this well requires you to understand the trappings of titles and know when to put on your title and when to put it aside which will then, in turn, powerfully inform how you speak up and listen up.

WHAT DOES THIS MEAN FOR HOW YOU SPEAK UP?

When we choose whether to say something or stay silent, we are perhaps consciously, but certainly unconsciously, labelling ourselves relative to others. We weigh up the balance of these labels and this gives us an indication of whether we are relatively powerful – or relatively weak – in a given situation. This can give us confidence or might make us doubt ourselves, which in turn has a knock-on effect on speaking up.

NIKKI AND RACHEL

Working with the board of a food retail organisation, we see this first hand. The head of HR, Nikki, is conscious of two labels in particular. First, she is the only woman on the board. Second, the label 'HR' does not hold much weight in her organisation where HR has connotations of 'fluffy people stuff', 'intangible', 'administration', whereas the real work is seen to be done by the operations and products teams. Acutely aware of being female and HR, Nikki has to work hard to have her voice heard. Gradually perceptions on the board are starting to change, but it takes time for such ingrained negative valence to alter and for Nikki to build confidence and find her voice.

The situation is completely different with a technology firm we work with. The board is split equally gender-wise. The head of HR, Rachel, is called 'Chief People Officer' and she is seen to have a critical role in shaping the organisation's strategy, which is wholly reliant on finding and keeping talented employees. She wears the label of her previous famous Silicon Valley employer, which is roundly admired by all, and she speaks up in the knowledge that her opinion counts.

---

1. What titles and labels do you give yourself?
2. What titles and labels do you give those with whom you work closely?
3. What do those labels convey in terms of relative status and authority?
4. Do the same labels convey different things in different settings? For example, does your job title stay the same but mean different things to you (and, you imagine, to others) in different working groups?

Our research suggests you need to pay particular attention to four consequences of titles in relation to speaking up. Some of them will sound familiar because they have been mentioned earlier:

- **Igniting the imposter syndrome:** The way we apply titles and labels is one key way we ignite the imposter syndrome. We think of ourselves as just a newbie, just a middle manager or just from the back office, and through the lower status we apply to ourselves (plus the relatively higher status we apply to everyone else), we convince ourselves that our opinion doesn't count or wouldn't be listened to. The labels can be even more ingrained and implicit: 'I am a woman therefore my career will always come second to family,' 'I am black, so they will never really feel comfortable with me (or me with them),' or 'I am old, so my mind isn't sharp any more.'

Ensuring the imposter syndrome doesn't subsume us requires us to spot our labelling and assumptions and to question them.

> Think back to a time where you have experienced the imposter syndrome. What were the titles and labels you placed on yourself and others and what were the consequences?

- **Discounting others or speaking over them:** In contrast to the imposter syndrome, if we label ourselves higher status and those around us lower, we can risk speaking up *too* much. Often our discounting of others is unconscious. If we are particularly mindful, we might spot thoughts such as 'Oh they won't add anything' or 'Well I know best here', or we might first spot emotions or sensations such as feeling frustrated when others start to speak or feeling excessively confident or even arrogant.

> 1. In what situations at work do you feel very confident about speaking up?
> 2. What role do titles and labels play in giving you this confidence?

- **Inappropriately trusting or distrusting others:** Based on the way we label people we can end up failing to challenge or challenging unfairly. Both of these can result in poor decisions and even in tragedy. As with the plane disasters, if we trust those senior to us too much, failing to call out mistakes can even lead to loss of life. Conversely, if we distrust someone because unconsciously they remind us of someone we distrusted in the past, we can ignore what they say and make the wrong decision. A male executive we worked with figured out that the wariness he experienced towards his new colleague – an older, physically large and loud man – was in part because he reminded him of his father with whom he had a difficult relationship.

1. Who do you trust and distrust at work?
2. Carefully try to decipher how much of this is down to hard evidence, and how much is down to the labels you apply to them.

■ **Accepting that sometimes, you need to stay silent.**

ROWAN WILLIAMS

Rowan Williams, when Archbishop of Canterbury, found himself with a formidable speak-up challenge. He travelled to Zimbabwe to present a dossier of human rights violations against Anglicans to the then president, Robert Mugabe. In his interview with Megan, he explained that he was aware that Mugabe would inevitably apply one devastating title to him, that of 'colonialist'. Mugabe was never going to permit any challenge on human rights from a colonialist. Rowan Williams therefore said that he purposely left it to Archbishop Thabo Makgoba from South Africa to lean forward and say 'President Mugabe, you call yourself a Christian. What do you think you are doing?'

When do the titles given to you by others (even if you don't agree with them) mean that you are not well placed to speak up? When might you instead need to support someone else to say something?

WHAT DOES THIS MEAN FOR HOW YOU LISTEN UP?

While this process of categorising ourselves and others naturally affects whether we choose to say something, it also affects whose opinion we seek and whom we listen to. Here are five consequences of titles that show up in our research that you need to watch out for:

■ **Helping our 'in-group':** If we are unaware of the positive valence we attach to certain titles and labels, we can end up subtly, and not so subtly, discriminating in favour of our in-group. In this way we are not so much being prejudiced *against* others in any overt way (openly disrespecting or expressing hostility); rather we are favouring those that are like ourselves.

The consequences of this absence of helping the 'out-group' though can be just as devastating. Banaji and Greenwald explain that in their studies 'in-group favouritism may be the largest contributing factor to the relative disadvantages experienced by Black Americans and other already disadvantaged groups'.[8] This form of discrimination is often hidden. It involves seeking out opinions from our in-group, inviting them to events, promoting them more quickly and introducing them to networks. And we often don't realise we are receiving benefits as a result of us being in the in-group (as described above in 'advantage blindness').

Alumni networks are a good example of how this in-group might help. The 'old boys' network' still conveys considerable advantages to its members.

1. When might you seek out opinions from those who are like you?
2. When might you hesitate before listening to advice given by those unlike you?

■ **Sticking to our 'little lists':** Linked to these in-group preferences, through labelling others as 'like us', we can tend to stick to the same person or group for advice. Earlier we introduced you to the CEO who told us that 'everyone's opinion counted', but then in the same breath said 'I do have my little list of who fits and who doesn't' and he was using his little list to determine whose views counted.

When we asked our survey respondents if they went to the same people for advice, a significant 62% stated that they did this usually or always. And it can be a valid strategy if you're a busy manager who simply doesn't have time to engage with people who might not have the expertise or understanding needed.

1. Do you tend to go to the same person or group for opinions and advice?
2. Might your shortcut unfairly silence some voices?
3. What might be the negative consequences for both you and those who are left out?

- **Being susceptible to 'truthiness':** Stephen Colbert, the American comedian, coined the phrase 'truthiness' to refer to our tendency to accept propositions that we want to believe without checking the evidence for them. The concept has been used in relation to both the American and British political scenes recently in debates examining the role of fake news and the general public's susceptibility to believing propaganda.

  Succumbing to truthiness is more likely if we have labelled the source of the information as 'good' or 'right'. Fred Goodwin, CEO of the Royal Bank of Scotland, became unchallengeable over time, with too many people wanting to believe his truth about the financial performance of the group, even when his model of operating had gone way beyond the bounds of what might be good for the bank or the sector.[9] Nearly every scandal we've referred to in this book has a pattern where people have wanted to believe what they've heard – and it has been in nobody's interest to rock the boat.

  So listening up well requires us to be discerning and notice if we are beginning to accept something someone says as truth without question.

> Whose opinion do you automatically trust?

- **The inflated value of the words of the great and good:** If a powerful person says something is interesting we can tend to inflate this into 'really worth pursuing – we need to action this', simply because we idolise their opinion. Or we hear 'I'm not convinced' and read that to mean 'it's a rubbish idea – definitely don't take it further'. We call this 'title inflation', the process through which, as a result of someone's title, their words are magnified and given more meaning than is helpful.

> 1. Whose words do you hang upon in this way?
> 2. Who might listen to you in this way?

- **We take agreement (or silence) as meaning we're right:** Listening up well means that we can't accept at face value when others agree with us – or assume agreement just because others don't challenge us. We have to realise that the titles placed on us can propel us into a relatively powerful position, which in turn means that others may be reticent to speak up.

When *The New York Times*[10] pummelled Amazon for the 'bruising culture' in its warehouses, CEO Jeff Bezos responded in a memo to staff saying that the article 'doesn't describe the Amazon I know'. As CEO however, even with the best of intentions, he would be unable to have a clear view of what was going on in every corner of his business. Just because he does not hear of problems does not mean there aren't any.

1. If you have a powerful title, what skilful questions do you ask to elicit meaningful feedback?
2. How do you invite others to challenge you safely?

An executive we worked with had a particularly useful question: 'What do you know that I need to know, but will never be told?'

SO WHAT SHOULD YOU DO?

In order to limit the negative consequences of applying titles to ourselves and others, try these things:

- **Spot the labelling you do:** Be aware of the consequent judgements as you are making them through developing mindfulness. Spotting judgements takes a lot more effort than making them.

- **Know the titles others apply to you and work with them:** If titles convey on you higher status or scariness and you need to hear challenge, then you could try to reduce the power distance between you and others to put others at their ease.

A very moving example of this is described by Banaji and Greenwald. The American journalist Brent Staples realises others apply to him the label of 'big, black man' which equates to dangerous and confesses to whistling popular pieces of classical music in public places to reassure passers-by to create an alternative Vivaldi = harmless association.

If titles convey lower status then you may need to seek alliances, credentialise and become politically more savvy.

- **Remove social labels from certain decision-making processes:** Recruitment and promotions are an obvious area. In 1970 the top five orchestras in the US had fewer than 5% women. Today this stands at more like 30%. In part, this increase is due to a change in the way instrumentalists are assessed – through the adoption of blind auditions. Musicians play behind a screen so that the judges cannot label them as a woman and unconsciously apply a negative evaluation as a result. This has been taken a step further and musicians are now asked to remove footwear as the sound of heels walking on to the stage was giving away gender.

  We need to consider how the metaphorical 'screen' can be put in place in some of our workplace processes. There are opportunities for doing this, for example, through taking out names and references to gender and race in job applications and in requests for grants and funding.[11]

  Does your workplace assess and publish statistics relating to the percentages of minorities achieving promotions or placements so that bias can be uncovered? What practices have been put into place or could be to reduce the impact of unconscious bias resulting from titles and labels?

- **Expose yourself to positive role models:** Unfortunately, increasing awareness of hidden biases does not get rid of them as they are just so deeply ingrained. This means that if we want to change our associations with certain titles we need to seek out evidence and subject our minds to that evidence over a sustained period of time. Banaji and Greenwald showed that minimal interventions just before decision-making can make a difference. For example, a study where participants viewed pictures of ten admirable black Americans and ten despicable white Americans led to weaker 'white = good' associations.[12] However, such changes are 'elastic', meaning that we revert back to our previous associations unless the exposure to alternative associations is continued.

  In the workplace context, there is a compelling reason for ensuring there are senior role models from minority groups. If there are female members on the board, for example, employees may over time increase their association 'female = leader'.

- **Embrace the positive potential of labels and titles:** Notice which titles are useful for people to know about you. In the case of

Megan's example of the man with his eight titles, maybe it would have been good if he'd stopped to think about the one or two that would be really useful for these people in this immediate situation to know about him.

KEY MESSAGES

- Giving people titles and labels is a fact of life and greatly influences who we judge worthy of speaking up to or listening to.

- Used well, titles provide people with context about where someone is coming from – and what is likely to count as truth to them.

- Seeing how we title and label people can be very uncomfortable, revealing that we have some pretty questionable ways of seeing our fellow human beings. However, we cannot escape the effect that innumerable social cues – stories, jokes, language, images – have on the formation of our unconscious biases.

- Titles can be a very good way of demarcating when we are shifting between personal and professional conversations – and formal and informal ones.

- Becoming conscious of how you title yourself and others is a vital first step to becoming better at engaging with a broader cross-section of society – and the knowledge this broader cross-section has.

- Unconscious bias will always be with you. The best you can do is follow the advice of the playwright Samuel Beckett and 'fail better'.

- Role models help us to develop different associations, such as woman = leader, and can be effective in sustainably changing unconscious biases.

If you do only one thing now, inquire with your team into the 'titles that count' – the social rules of who gets heard – and then figure out together what you're going to do about it.

NOTES

1. See the excellent book: Banaji, M. and Greenwald, A. (2013) *Blindspot: Hidden Biases of Good People.* Random House.
2. https://hbr.org/2003/12/how-unethical-are-you
3. https://implicit.harvard.edu/implicit/
4. *Blindspot,* p. 56.
5. www.linkedin.com/pulse/can-we-talk-power-ben-fuchs/
6. https://hbr.org/2018/04/do-you-have-advantage-blindness
7. Wellcome Trust – see www.mhj.org.uk
8. *Blindspot,* p. 162.
9. For more on this read: Iain Martin (2014) '*Fred Goodwin, RBS and The Men Who Blew up the British economy',* Simon & Schuster UK.
10. https://www.nytimes.com/2015/08/16/technology/inside-amazon-wrestling-big-ideas-in-a-bruisingworkplace.html
11. https://www.theguardian.com/women-in-leadership/2013/oct/14/blind-auditions-orchestras-gender-bias
12. *Blindspot,* p. 152.

CHAPTER 6

HOW-TO: SPEAK UP AND LISTEN UP WITH SKILL

Here we help you pull together a plan of campaign for how to create a better speak-up, listen-up culture for you and your organisation. It's about the pragmatic choices you make and actions you take to help you and others speak up and listen up effectively. It's the strategies and tactics you use for your next conversation and for helping future conversations happen.

You will learn:

- to see speaking up and listening up as a social dance – and not just a solo performance
- the pragmatic 'how-tos' of speaking up and listening up most effectively, the questions to ask yourself and the traps to watch out for
- how to develop the mindful attention and awareness that underpins your capacity to know what to do, when and how
- how to build the psychological safety in your workplace that can facilitate a speak-up, listen-up culture.

We start by examining the why, who, what, where and when of speaking up and provide a checklist to work through for good measure. We list the top traps to keep an eye out for. Then we do the same for listening up.

Checklists can be very useful tools in your kit bag, but used without attention, awareness and discernment they become ineffectual, even counterproductive – and the workplace is awash with badly used tools. To avoid this, you need the capacity for mindfulness. We will explain how you can train your mind to be more thoughtful, considered and skilful in your speaking up and listening up choices and actions.

We also turn to the contextual challenge of creating *group* transparency, examining the vital need for psychological safety and exploring how that develops through strong processes for reflection, feedback, practice, recognition and diversity.

PULLING IT ALL TOGETHER – HOW TO SPEAK UP

Speaking up *so we will be heard* requires two very tricky (and often underrated) skills.

The first is self-awareness: knowing our values, patterns of behaviour and current emotional state as well as our assumptions and judgements of others.

The second is empathy and a capacity to see the world from the shoes of the person we are speaking up to. Empathy is problematic because when we want to speak up, particularly when we are about to challenge the predominant discourse, we often become very self-focused.

An 'amygdala hijack' is when the part of our brain responsible for emotions and survival instinct kicks in to the extent that we short-cut our rational, thoughtful brain and become overwhelmed with fight, flight or freeze reactions. When we perceive danger – as we often do when we are about to speak up – we can experience narrowing perspective, breathlessness and heightened emotions such as anger or fear.

Self-awareness goes out the window as we find ourselves on automatic survival mode which renders us incapable of empathising.

Yet, ironically, it is self-awareness and empathy that will probably lead us to speak up in a way that most safeguards our survival – coming out with our reputation and relationships intact. This is where rehearsing and seeking advice is so important. Admittedly, we can't always prepare and sometimes we have to respond in the moment, but even then it is helpful to have some sort of process that reminds us, before we criticise or offer an idea which goes against the grain, to link into our intention and values and step into the other person's shoes, if only for a few seconds.

The 5Ws gives us a process for interrogating ourselves, inquiring into the other person's perspective and exploring our context before and as we speak up. We describe this below along with key questions which can serve as a checklist:

- **Why** examines the purpose behind you speaking up. It asks what outcome you are seeking and what your positive intention is. It can be easy to speak up with a superficial, immediate need to blame or complain. Sometimes we want to speak so that we'll be seen and recognised by someone we perceive as important. On reflection though, what you might actually be seeking in the 'big picture' is a win–win process that helps two departments work well together and both succeed.

Earlier we looked at the Canadian CEO who had to let go of the habit of blaming the bearers of bad news, a habit she'd learnt from her angry mother. Her motivation to speak up shifted from the desire to blame to the desire to support collective inquiry.

1. Why do you want to speak up and what outcome are you looking for?
2. Does it really matter whether you speak up or not? For you? For others?
3. How do you want people to feel once you've said your piece?

- **Who** identifies the right person or people to speak to and whether it is *you* that is best placed to speak up. The person we may *want* to talk to may not be the person we *need* to in order to effect change.

Our habit of reshuffling our organisational structure compounds the complexity of finding who is responsible for what. It can interfere with our understanding of politics and titles, which is vital in deciphering who is the most appropriate person to speak to and whether it should be you or someone else that speaks up.

Earlier we described how Rowan Williams, ex-Archbishop of Canterbury, decided, although he wanted to challenge Robert Mugabe, that he wasn't the right person to because of his title of colonialist. On the other hand, we have also highlighted our tendency to abdicate – and assume it must be someone else's job to speak up, not in a thoughtful effort to be effective, but in an effort to avoid responsibility.

> 1. Who, given their agenda, is willing to listen to you?
> 2. Who has the power to act on what you say and support you?
> 3. Are you the person who can and should speak up?

- **Where** identifies the location that would be most conducive to speaking up and being heard. Environment matters, so determining whether it is likely to be most effective in a formal place like an office, or informally while outside the office, is important. Is what you have to communicate best done via email, on a virtual platform or face to face? What works best for the *other person*?

We often facilitate 'walk and talks' in leadership workshops as walking side by side in the open air can be less intimidating. Sometimes just changing the place can change who says what to whom.

On a Scottish university campus the head of one department repurposed a gardener's shed and kitted it out with comfy chairs and a woodburner. It became a place where academics, students and managers could come together to have different types of conversation.

> 1. Where are you going to feel most able to speak. . . and they to listen?
> 2. Should this conversation be private, or do you need to have some people with you (or in earshot)?
> 3. What's the best medium for this conversation? Virtual? Face to face? Phone?

- **When** identifies when the other person can best hear you. Timing is what makes or kills a joke. The same applies for speaking up. Sometimes you might need to speak up when others are around. At other times, you might be more likely to be heard in a one-to-one conversation. Now might be the right time for *you*, but if you can see that the other person is stressed or busy you might need to rethink.

We know that many important conversations happen outside formal work hours. The deputy chairman from earlier specifically chose to challenge the chairman when they were travelling and they were enjoying a glass of wine in the evening.

At a London cancer hospital, the constant pressure on costs had led to the elimination of all unused space. Senior nurses had nowhere to go for that timely, private word with a member of staff when they saw them doing something that wasn't quite right. Everything fell into a formal process, where conversations were scheduled for some future time, when the exact details would be dependent on what got written down and relied on contested memories.

---

1. When do you need to have this conversation? Right now? This week? Next month?

2. When will you be at your best speaking up? Do you need to cool off, or is it better that you have the conversation with fire in your belly?

3. When will the other person be open to listen?

■ **What** refers to the precise words and signals you should use to get your message across. Your words may spark the interest of the other person or may provoke them to jump to negative conclusions. Your body language and tone might need to change in order to emphasise curiosity rather than communicate blame.

What requires you to consider the cultural context – what etiquette do you need to follow?

An aid worker in Sierra Leone learned to use a softening form of words when asking people to produce things for him. To get a late report produced he would say: 'I would like to hope the report would be on my desk by tomorrow evening', to which the reply was: 'I also would like to hope that the report would be with you.' Not a form of exchange that would work on Wall Street, but then Wall Street directness would be counter-productive in Sierra Leone.

---

1. What exactly are you going to say and what key phrases or questions will you need to use?

2. Given your understanding of the other person's context, personality and perspective, what signals should you send verbally and non-verbally and what should you avoid?

3. How will you judge if your speaking up has been a success?

WATCH OUT FOR THESE SPEAK-UP TRAPS

Here are three of the most common traps we fall into when trying to speak up effectively:

■ **We doubt ourselves:** The imposter syndrome strikes and we undermine our confidence by telling ourselves that our opinion doesn't really count for much, we're rubbish at speaking up or someone else would be far better at saying something, so we'll leave it. We have talked about tackling the imposter syndrome. The first step is to hear that internal voice of doubt when it arises, to question it and remind ourselves of times when we have spoken up effectively.

■ **We abdicate:** We consider speaking up and then we decide it isn't our responsibility. This could be either because we think it is someone else's job to say something (someone more senior or the regulator), or because nothing will happen anyway so therefore there is no point in even trying. Although these thought processes might be valid in some cases, we have found that they are over-used and often serve to help ourselves feel better about remaining a bystander. To interrupt this habit, we need once again to take a long, hard look at our assumptions and question them. We need to ask ourselves whether staying silent is wise, appropriate, ethical, irresponsible or lazy.

■ **We speak in a way that suits us, rather than the other person:** This is perhaps most apparent when we are speaking to someone from a different cultural background. We assume they will want to hear about a problem or an idea in the same way that we would – in the same place, at the same time, in the same manner. It may be common sense that if you are from the UK and you need to challenge a Chinese leader you might think through the cultural norms of how that needs to be done – but common sense can be very uncommon in the workplace.

We can also tend to speak up at a time and place when *we* want to and are ready to, without thinking about the time and place that would work best for the other person. The message with this trap is that it is imperative to remember to empathise – to imagine the world from the point of view of the person you want to talk to. Again, the 5Ws checklist may help you to do that. Even a few minutes of preparation can make a huge difference to the outcome of a conversation.

PULLING IT ALL TOGETHER – HOW TO LISTEN UP

Listening up is a blind spot for most of us. We think we do it well but our biggest downfall is that we ignore or underestimate the silencing effect of power distance – the extent to which less powerful individuals accept and expect power inequality.

We consider ourselves approachable and we ask people to speak up – and then think it is their fault if they don't. An invaluable capacity once again here is empathy. In order to really skilfully invite another person to speak up, we need to be able to step into their shoes and figure out what we can do to help them to be most at ease. We then need to seek feedback from trusted advisors (who won't just tell us that we're marvellous) in order to learn and improve. This is a lifetime's work, as we discover what and who we are prone to listen to and what and who we tend to dismiss as irrelevant.

Once again, we will use the 5Ws to help us to consider listening up thoroughly.

- **Why** reinforces the commitment you need to listen up well. It reminds you of the importance of helping others speak up – and the consequences of them staying silent. It may remind you of the business imperative to hear about misconduct or to hear important ideas.

  In the case of the founder of the recruitment firm, the 'why' of listening to the youngest monk in the monastery was rooted in a moral instruction that listening to people is part of being an ethical human being and leader.

  Why comes down to whether or not you *really* value the opinion of others. Our belief that as the boss we must already have the answers (and therefore not seek them from others) is deeply ingrained.

  In conversation with an ex-CEO, John was jokingly told that the 'point of being a CEO was so you didn't have to listen to people'. It can be a completely new mind and skillset for us to learn why we need to inquire and listen as leaders.

---

1. What are your areas of ignorance?
2. Why and how are outcomes different when you are listening to learn rather than to instruct, correct or win?
3. What do you want to know that you don't currently know?

- **Who** helps you to identify those voices that you really want and need to hear. Reflecting on this might illuminate who you tend to feel comfortable listening to, who you take for granted and who you tend to discount or avoid.

During a banking merger, senior management were surprised when a number of key staff resigned. No one had got round to telling them about their future and the bonuses they were going to receive as management were too busy with restructuring plans to hear their concerns until it was too late. We spoke to the CEO who liked people to 'be bright, be quick, be gone'. She had to learn that if she didn't give people with more roundabout communication styles the time and space to feel comfortable with her, they would stay silent and she would miss out on important ideas.

This links to the challenge of unconscious bias we have examined. Our attachment to beliefs and practices about whose opinion really counts amplifies some voices and diminishes others.

1. Who do you go to in order to hear something useful, different or uncomfortable?
2. How have you widened or changed who you listen to in the last year?
3. Who are you instinctively biased towards and against (even if you wish you weren't)?

- **Where** identifies the environment that would be most conducive for the other person to speak freely. For example, is the department or organisation-wide meeting a likely place for good feedback or questions? Is an invitation to an anonymous, virtual platform better to elicit ideas than face to face? Is a coffee outside the workplace more likely to put someone else at their ease?

A senior civil servant we worked with had instituted that as many meetings as possible took place while completing a walk around one of the London park lakes. In practice, this meant the business aspect of the meeting tended to be done by about three-quarters of a lap, leaving them room to connect more personally for the last quarter. It created time to build empathy and deepen relationships.

Earlier we reported on the European engineering CEO frustrated when no one asked any questions at a town hall (large group) meeting.

Ironically, the meeting had been arranged to address complaints about how people felt unable to ask questions of senior leaders. If we are of high rank and status it is all too easy to forget how intimidating public settings can be and that means we must choose locations that do not reinforce our power or others' powerlessness.

---

1. Where's the best place to meet people so they'll feel comfortable speaking up to you?

2. Do people have a choice of media or environment where they can talk to you?

3. Where do you feel most ready and able to hear what people say?

- **When** helps you to choose the right moment to invite someone to speak up – when both they and you have the time to consider things.

  In one organisation the regulator was due to visit to determine whether to grant an important accreditation. The organisation planned the agenda so that the regulator would meet with small groups of employees. But the regulator insisted that she saw each person individually, aware that in this context asking people to tell their truth in a group of colleagues was more challenging than in a one-to-one meeting.

  In our initial research interviews, it was not unusual to be given an interview date in three to six months' time. 'Busyness' was the normal reason given for this. To listen to people you have to keep yourself free enough so that people can get hold of you at a time that works for them. This takes extraordinary discipline in the workplace where we lionise meetings, working lunches, staying late and generally using every moment of our day.

---

1. When in your diary or schedule is there space for spontaneous conversations?

2. Does how and when you are available reflect *your* needs or the needs of those who might want to speak to you?

3. Do normal meetings have enough slack in them for others to reflect, inquire, challenge and offer new ideas?

■ *What* asks you to choose the most appropriate language – verbal and non-verbal – when inviting someone to speak up. The difference that skilful questions can make can be enormous. One of the best questions we heard used by a manager was 'What do you know that I need to know (but won't be told)?'

If you are wearing a frown on your face you may be sending signals that silence others. If you hog most of the airtime in a meeting and tend to advocate rather than ask any questions, you shouldn't be surprised when good ideas cease to flow.

What also pays attention to what we seek information on and what we filter out and have learnt to discount. A big challenge for many managers is being in the grip of the 'tyranny of the tangible' and solutions. Inviting and then listening to people who are speaking about personal feelings, subjective realities and situations that can't be readily fixed is rare.

> 1. What's your reaction to being challenged?
> 2. What do you do to make others feel important, comfortable and significant?
> 3. How do you phrase your questions in ways that help people to open up?

WATCH OUT FOR THESE LISTEN-UP TRAPS

Here are three of the most common listening-up traps we have encountered in our research. For more on these, listen to Megan's TEDx talk called 'How your Power Silences Truth'.[1]

■ **We forget how scary we are:** We think we are lovely and approachable, but even if we are, our job title, network, personality, background or appearance may render us more powerful and therefore intimidating to others. Our research shows that many of us are completely blind to this – or we underestimate it – and we therefore imagine that people are speaking up to us and we are getting to hear the truth. Our survey results tell us that a huge 80%, 75% and 66% of respondents felt those more senior, peers and those more junior, respectively, would *never* or *rarely* consider them as scary. This is a serious blind spot.

■ **We don't question our 'little list' of whose opinion counts:** As with our CEO who admitted to having a little list of who he felt fitted in his organisation and who he felt didn't, we all have conscious and unconscious lists of whose opinion we want to seek out and whose we will discount. These lists are informed by the titles and labels that we place on others. Some of the judgements that relate to age, gender, race and appearance cannot fail to impact who we listen to. So, we need to pay attention to those little lists and question them – a lot.

- **We send 'shut-up' signals, not 'speak-up' ones:** Other people look at us, weigh up our body language and our tone of voice and determine whether it is safe to speak up or not. They may make misjudgements here – they may not realise that our deep frown is our 'thinking face'. It is our responsibility to 'know our face' and what it is communicating to others – and to change it if needed. We may generally be great at this, but unfortunately it is that time where we lose our temper with someone, or cut them off impatiently, that will be talked about. Stories like that silence people. So we have to be mindful of our signals and quickly make amends when we get it wrong.

SPEAKING AND LISTENING UP *MINDFULLY*

We hope you find the 5Ws and the checklist questions useful and that the examples we have used inspire you to try different ways to speak up and listen up well. However, there are no one-size-fits-all solutions. To use these ideas effectively we need to come to them with the right attitude and attention.

It's a bit like buying an Ikea flat-packed desk, setting it out on your floor and picking up the instruction manual. The manual might be helpful – even straightforward – but if we approach it with the wrong mindset ('I'm useless at this, this is going to be really frustrating' or 'I'm not sure I can be bothered with all this'), then the manual is probably not going to be employed in the best way and will have limited use.

Speaking up and listening up well is founded upon on our ability to choose to pay attention to our state, our environment and the other person and spot how this all changes moment by moment. We must have an ability to see things from the perspective of other people and regulate our emotions so that we can choose the right response (rather than react through automatic habits). We also need to be able to both listen *and* speak well in the same conversation, carefully discerning when we need to speak and when we need to listen.

We must therefore have the ability to pay attention on purpose in each present moment with an attitude of care and compassion. We call this capacity mindfulness.

Megan's research with Michael Chaskalson[2] has uncovered three key components to mindfulness – allowing, inquiry and meta-awareness – called AIM for short,[3] all of which are highly relevant to speaking and listening up. Here they are.

- **Allowing:** Allowing means we accept that 'what is the case is the case'. In our conversations we spend a considerable amount of time wishing things were different to how they are. 'I wish I hadn't just said that,' 'I wish they listened better,' 'I wish they'd just get to the point' and 'I wish my department had a better reputation so people would listen to me.'

  Allowing may mean accepting that in this moment our boss *is* like they are, the systems in place *are* as they are and discrimination *is* as it is. Similarly, we need to allow that we are human and have emotions and make mistakes. We may wish we hadn't said what we'd said and we may wish we didn't feel anxious and think we shouldn't, but it *is* what it is.

  Allowing doesn't mean we won't try and change things or learn and develop. However, *right now,* passionately saying to ourselves 'It's not fair,' 'This shouldn't have happened,' 'They shouldn't be like that,' 'I don't want this' and 'I'm useless' may not enable us to move forwards productively and skilfully. Rather, thinking to ourselves 'This is what the situation is right now – so given that, how can I best move forwards?' keeps us in a more generative, open-minded mode from where we can respond more thoughtfully.

- **Inquiry:** Inquiry means we are curious about our experience, the experience of others and the particular context we are situated within. Without it we stay hypnotised by our own unquestioned perspective and our speaking and listening up is restricted and partial. Inquiry can move us from a position where we are thinking 'I'm right, they just need to listen' to 'What assumptions am I making here and what might things look like from their perspective?' It can move us from 'I'm just going to stay silent' to 'If I were to speak up effectively, how would I do that?'

Learning and development is founded on our ability to be interested in something, go out and explore it, reflect on what we find and develop actions to continue our experimentation. This cycle of questioning, experimentation and reflection is known as 'action inquiry' and it is one of the best methods, at both individual and group levels, for instigating sustainable changes to the habits of what we say and how we listen. It is often our first port of call when we advise individuals and teams how to alter their conversational habits.

■ **Meta-awareness:** Meta-awareness refers to our unique ability to observe our thoughts, emotions, sensations and impulses as we are experiencing them, rather than being so caught up in them that we are driven to react in automatic ways. When we are in the middle of a heated debate, it is this capacity that allows us to see ourselves in action and make considered changes to the signals we are sending, or re-frame our internal dialogue away from frustration and towards curiosity.

If we are about to blurt something out because we are overcome by emotion; if we are in the process of standing by silent while a colleague is harassed; if we are happily advocating away without asking the other person what they think or giving them a moment to speak; or if we are discounting the person who has entered our office before they have even had a chance to say anything, it is meta-awareness that enables us to stop, observe our habits and choose a different course of action.

Nothing about the way you speak or listen up will change unless you have this capacity.

PRACTISING 'MIND TIME'

Practices that develop allowing, inquiry and meta-awareness habits are likely to improve the way you speak and listen up to others. Megan and Michael's research indicates that one way of developing AIM is through practising 'mind time', or meditations, for ten minutes[4] or more a day (which is about 1% of your waking hours). They have shown that this can lead to significant improvements in our capacity to empathise with others, keep our focus on something without being distracted and feel more comfortable and confident in uncertain contexts.

Present moment awareness profoundly enables us to make the most appropriate choices when responding to people as we speak up or listen up to them. Without it, it simply does not occur to us to ask the 5W questions. We are too busy habitually reacting on autopilot to our situation.

That's why we train individuals and teams to be more mindful in order to give them the impetus and the opportunity to *notice* and then *alter* their habits of speaking and listening.

PSYCHOLOGICAL SAFETY

We might be tempted to examine 'how-to' from just an individual's perspective – how *you* speak up, how *you* listen up – but this is the place to remind ourselves that speaking up in teams and organisations is *relational*. It is a collective phenomenon.

Improving how we speak up and listen up in the workplace is primarily a social change. Our gestures and decisions have consequences on others and our choices are influenced by the actions of those around us. We are all engaged in an intricate dance where we follow and are followed by others. It is not a simple matter of an individual taking responsibility to speak up better. It is not the case that an individual's choice to stay silent only affects them. The reverberations are felt throughout the system.

So if you are charged, formally or informally, with improving transparency and dialogue in your workplace, you need to work with individuals (including yourself) *and* the system that surrounds them, helping people to learn how to speak up *and* to listen up. Without listening there is no speaking and without speaking there is no listening.

Psychological safety is the shared belief held by members of a team that the team is safe for interpersonal risk-taking.[5] Harvard professor, Amy Edmondson, has been instrumental in researching and advising how it is created (and destroyed) in groups. Using her and our own work we have identified five processes that help create the necessary safety for organisational openness and transparency:

■ Processes for **reflection** instigate pauses into a system so that we can understand something better and come up with appropriate responses.

  We facilitate processes of action inquiry (mentioned above) in the organisations we work with. Groups reflect on their speaking and listening up habits and come up with experiments for improvement.

Then they come back a few weeks later to discuss what happened, reflect on what they have learnt and what the next experiment might look like. It is through this cyclical process of reflection and action that we have seen sustainable change in a system instigated.

1. When do you and others get a chance to reflect on how you communicate with one another?
2. When do you deeply consider what it takes to encourage people to voice concerns and ideas?
3. How do you keep considering this over time, learning and improving?

■ Processes for **feedback** provide the means for individuals and teams to gather evidence and ideas about how to speak and listen up. This might mean enabling individuals and teams to access coaches and mentors who can give candid feedback and who might say things that others are too afraid to. Feedback might also include observation, recording and measurement.

We run our Speaking Truth to Power Culture survey[6] for organisations wanting to gather measurable feedback on their culture. The results are shared, discussed and an action inquiry approach, described above, is initiated.

1. Who can you go to, to get feedback?
2. Who will tell it to you straight?
3. How do you get alternative, challenging perspectives on your team or organisational culture?
4. If you think it all seems fine, how would you rigorously check that out?

■ Processes for **practice** might include working with actors (or trusted advisors) to rehearse ways of speaking and listening up.

We ask individuals to choose a real, difficult conversation that they should or need to have and, with a small number of colleagues observing, they practise their conversation with a trained actor. They receive feedback and get a chance to run the conversation again, differently. It is persistently rated as a highly significant and impactful learning experience.

At a group level, we enable practice by facilitating a team through different ways of communicating and challenging with one another – stopping and starting the action in order to reflect, learn and ensure mistakes are allowed and indeed encouraged. For example, we might hand out a devil's advocate card to individuals who then have to practise challenging decisions (and are invited to be imperfect and learn through the process). Or we might pause proceedings to inquire confidentially with individuals, one to one, what they are choosing to say and what elephants in the room remain. Then the collective patterns and elephants are brought back to the group and discussed safely but rigorously.

1. Do you have a place to practise different ways of communicating?
2. Do you have people you can turn to who will listen to you and help you to practise?
3. When, in your team, do you create the circumstances where you can communicate differently, make mistakes, experiment some more and learn?

- Processes for **recognition** ensure that speaking up and listening up are formally and informally appreciated and recognised. Importantly, this means not punishing – and indeed celebrating – mistakes (as long as there is learning from them). It means amplifying positive stories and noticing when stories are negative and silencing.

Through ethnographic studies we observe groups interacting and talk with them in order to see the world from their perspective. This enables us to highlight the stories, patterns and games that expose what really gets rewarded and punished, but rarely gets questioned. We can spot the 'competing commitments' which may encourage speaking and listening up on the one hand and discourage it on the other. For example, we mentioned earlier the organisation that listed 'positive about change' as a corporate value. This had been translated into 'don't say anything that might be considered negative' and in turn was seen to undermine their other quoted corporate value: transparency.

1. Who gets recognised in your organisation and why?
2. What behaviour is really being encouraged and prioritised?
3. What happens if you make a mistake in your speaking up or listening up?
4. What stories exist about people who have spoken up in the past?

■ Processes for **diversity** ensure there is access to a variety of perspectives and that those voices are invited (safely) and appreciated. Recruitment and promotion processes play a key role in ensuring that an organisation is not focused solely on its own likeness.

Megan recently met with a group of Danish high performers: 30 white males in their early forties, many of whom were dressed the same. Nobody else noticed or commented on the conformity so Megan brought it to the attention of the group and facilitated a conversation as to the consequences of such homogeneity.

We use psychometric instruments to uncover cognitive diversity[7] and help groups to appreciate difference and discuss what was once hidden and taken for granted. We uncover unconscious bias through our research on titles and use our survey to scrutinise people's persistent denial that they discriminate.

---

1. Look around your team. Are they like you?
2. To what extent do you have genuinely different perspectives being offered in your workplace?
3. How might unconscious bias sneak into your recruitment, development and retention processes?

Our voice is discretionary. Staying silent is the rational thing to do if the consequences of speaking up are dangerous. Psychological safety is the vital backdrop to creating transparency, experimentation and disruption.

If we don't feel safe we don't speak up. If we don't speak up, others will gradually learn to follow suit. Then before you know it, there is a culture of silence which can be unpicked – but only with a great deal of patience, commitment and care.

To discover how to help ourselves and others speak and listen up well, we must examine and seek to change *both* our individual *and* our collective habits.

KEY MESSAGES

■ There is no single right way to speak or listen up – no perfect 'how-to'. What will work for you depends on your personal, interpersonal and professional power – and the culture, the established norms and practices of the workplace you are part of.

- Self-awareness and empathy are critical in developing the effectiveness of how we speak and listen up.

- Reflecting on the 5Ws – why, who, where, when and what – of speaking up and listening up helps us to empathise and connect better with each other.

- To connect well with each other requires us to be mindful – to pay attention to ourselves and others, in the present moment, with care.

- Psychological safety is imperative if you are to create an environment in your team and organisation conducive to speaking and listening up. You need to focus on processes for reflection, feedback, practice, recognition and diversity.

- Speaking up and listening up happens between people. It is a social activity and therefore we need to work at a group level to create safety, *as well* as at the individual competency level.

If you do only one thing now, think of something challenging that you need to say. Rehearse with someone before the next meeting when you want to be heard.

NOTES

1. https://www.youtube.com/watch?v=Sq475Us1KXg
2. See https://hbr.org/2016/12/how-to-bring-mindfulness-to-your-companys-leadership and https://hbr.org/2016/11/mindfulness-works-but-only-if-you-work-at-it
3. Chaskalson, M. and Reitz, M. (2018) *Mind Time: How Ten Mindful Minutes Can Enhance Your Life, Work and Happiness.* Harper Thorson.
4. See www.mindtime.me for example meditations.
5. Edmondson, A. (1999) Psychological safety and learning behavior in work teams. *Administrative Science Quarterly,* 44, (2, June) (Jun., 1999), 350–383.
6. https://hultbusinessschool.eu.qualtrics.com/jfe/form/SV_a9uXunK7VUx0Yst.
7. https://hbr.org/2017/03/teams-solve-problems-faster-when-theyre-more-cognitively-diverse

CHAPTER 7

TRUTH IN THE FUTURE: THE PROFOUND CONSEQUENCES OF A DIGITAL WORLD

We now find ourselves in a rapidly changing environment where technological advancements are vying to influence our mind and our choices like never before. We are in a world where algorithms, which present certain information while hiding other data, mediate our perceptions about the world around us. Power is being defined more and more as those with access to technological resources, and those without, and those who are in a position to determine the application of these resources, and those who simply consume what others provide.

For better or for worse, our perspectives on TRUTH are being altered through our relative access and engagement with data, our knowledge of what lies behind this data and our capacity to discern what is real from what is fake. And things are only going to move faster with the exponential growth in technologies transforming the scope and scale of the digital world.

This book would not be complete therefore without considering the ways in which our choices about speaking up and listening up might be radically influenced in the future.

Of course, no one knows what the future is going to be like, even though we can be seduced by those who like to sell certainty. As a society we will construct that future together through the choices we *make, and don't make, living with the consequences, both intended and unintended.*

You will:

- *learn about some of the technological advancements that are likely to change the way we communicate.*

- *feel hope or despair (depending on your attitude) about the extraordinary possibilities that lie ahead of us.*

- *be able to position what you have learnt in the rest of this book into the radically changing wider societal context.*

- *consider (we hope) that continuing to develop your capacity to speak up and listen up will be more, rather than less, important in the future.*

TRUTH IN THE FUTURE: FOR BETTER OR FOR WORSE?

We wrote this book to help you to improve the effectiveness of how you speak up and listen up. By now, you should know the key issues that you navigate when you are in conversation: how much you trust in your own and others' opinions; how risky you think it is to speak up; how you understand and fathom the political environment of status, authority and personal agendas; the titles and labels you give yourself and others that communicate relative power; and the strategies – the 'how-to' – of moment-by-moment interaction.

You navigate these complex areas in your mind. You sift through your life experiences of relating to other people, take stock of your environment, examine the responses you get from your gestures and make judgements about what they mean. Then you will act (even if that act is to do nothing).

The world ahead of us is full of potential for changing and improving the way we meet, think, understand, care and decide. Few aspects of the way humans relate to one another will remain untouched by digital technology. We will be forced to think hard about what we want from our relationships with each other, or else allow technology providers to persuade us into new relational rules that fit more with their agendas.

For millennia we have developed age-old customs for reading and understanding each other and ourselves. Now, however, we are going to have to learn to work effectively *and ethically* with an additional vocabulary, in an explosion of data and new technology applications.

Knowledge about ourselves, each other and our relationships is likely to become more visible – and so more manageable, controllable and adaptable – than at any stage of human development. We just hope our moral and ethical intelligence is going to be able to keep up with the technical capabilities of this brave new world – a world where there are both extraordinarily inspiring possibilities and terrifying scenarios to be seriously contemplated and navigated.

We start by briefly explaining some terms and then, rather than claiming to have the truth about the future, we've created a range of scenarios based on an extrapolation of existing trends in the worlds of technology, politics and society at large and through interviewing individuals at the leading edge of technical innovation. Finally, we will discuss the possible implications on TRUTH, inviting you to consider a number of questions which will help you to figure out what all this could mean for you, your team and your workplace.

A NEW LANGUAGE: AN ARTIFICIAL, AUGMENTED AND ALGORITHMIC WORLD

Our technological future is described in a myriad of new words which can feel confusing. Indeed, there is a divide developing between those that speak this new language and those that do not: a difference in power and authority which holds implications already for how we speak up and who we listen to. It is not our aim here to describe everything from machine learning to autonomous architecture (other books already do this well), but we do refer to the three 'As' frequently and so we will at least get a bit clearer on those.

Groth and Nitzberg, in their book '*Solomon's Code*',[1] provide a useful and clear definition of *artificial intelligence* (AI): 'In the broadest sense, artificial intelligence is the capacity of machines to learn, reason, plan, and perceive; the primary traits we identify with human cognition (but, notably, not with consciousness or conscience).'

AI processes data but also learns as it does so that it becomes exponentially more advanced as time goes on. Newsfeeds on Facebook, Apple's 'Siri', Google search results and facial recognition technology are all examples of AI advances. Hannah Fry, Associate Professor in the Mathematics of Cities at University College London, urges us to use the phrase 'computational statistics' (CS) instead of AI because it may reduce the possibility of seeing AI as magic and instead remind us that it is very much shaped by human beings and our choices.

How AI/CS gets used is, and will continue to be, a function of how those with power seek to use it – and it will be a battleground for competing visions of the future. Some would argue we need to pay attention to JK Rowling here and her character Arthur Weasley in the Harry Potter series: 'Never trust anything that can think for itself if you can't see where it keeps its brain.'[2]

Augmented reality (AR) transforms volumes of data and analytics into images or animations that are overlaid on the real world.[3] We have become used to accessing information in 2D and attempting to translate this into our 3D world (the iconic scene of someone quizzically looking at a set of furniture instructions and then looking at the very real pieces sat in front of them on the floor), but now AR removes the translation bit of this process by bringing physical and digital data together to be processed simultaneously. Smart glasses used in manufacturing contexts to overlay instructions on to the physical machine are an example of one AR application.

An *algorithm* is a computer procedure that solves a problem by analysing data through following a number of specified steps. An example of algorithms are those used by Google to determine the ranked results in response to our search requests. Our preferences are tracked online and using that data organisations such as Facebook and Google use algorithms to determine what information to show us and what not to.[4] Decisions are made for us by code which is invisible to us. Facebook in particular has been in a maelstrom of controversy around how their algorithms have presented news feeds. These amplify to users some opinions and make others disappear and have been susceptible to foreign interference aiming to influence elections.

So how might AI, AR and the pervasive use of algorithms continue to shape the way we speak up and listen up?

SIX SCENARIOS FOR THE FUTURE

Let's peer into our possible future. Below are six scenarios presented as a means to fire your imagination and enable you to consider some of the possible impending consequences to the way you will speak and listen. Some of them describe situations which might be more likely and widespread and others might perhaps be more surprising and restricted (though we have no way of knowing).

1. Nowhere to hide – power steps out of the shadows

Around your (virtual) boardroom, you and your peers are interacting with smart glasses, contact lenses and devices which reveal both your own emotional state and that of your colleagues around the table. Your language is scrutinised to see how charged the words you are using are. Your meetings are refereed according to policies on who should get the airtime and who must not be ignored. Semantic analysis tools reveal the mix of advocacy and inquiry being used in any conversation. Your personal 'bot' warns you when it judges you to be leaning too far towards one side or the other.

You can see people's levels of fear and anxiety – and they can see yours – and that data is used as a proxy for a power-distance map. Who has the confidence right now is seen as powerful and who doesn't, less so. However, the utopian view of 'leader as all-knowing and infallible' has had to be questioned. The inevitability and ubiquity of vulnerability is acknowledged and out in the open.

Power, in terms of voice and impact, can no longer be wished away or ignored. Your implicit or tacit feel for who has most airtime, who wields power and influence, is now buttressed by data that is in the public domain. Power is more explicit. For some this is an invitation to revel in a 'might is right' approach to conversations, to figure out how to instil fear and compliance (but at least in these cases there is no place for claiming one thing while doing another). For others it allows power to be acknowledged and therefore used well so that the unconsciously powerful don't dominate conversations, and those who feel powerless no longer have their reality ignored.

How *you* use it, relies a great deal on your values and ethical choices.

2. Gaming the algorithm – a new world of fake-believe

As your words, spoken and written, expressed and unexpressed, become part of the public domain, it becomes all but impossible to hide from the consequences of what you say. How you are seen and how you see others emerges from the assumptions underpinning the myriad of algorithms that sift through the world of hard and soft data that tracks your every move.

If you are savvy, you present yourself in a way that fits with the algorithms that evaluate and rank your qualities. In order to demonstrate your commitment to your professional life you take care to belong to some chatrooms and online groups and not others, the modern-day equivalent of political networking – being at some meetings and not others.

New technology enables you to make sure that you are seen to contribute to the most influential online conversations in your workplace and that your contributions fit with the categories valued by the company algorithms which track you. You manage your conversational life to fit with the ideals assumed to be good in the eyes of those who devised the rules of the algorithm. Algorithms are invented to mitigate the influence of other algorithms. Technology steers your learning towards the use of some words in some places and not others as you game the system.

The Chinese social equivalent of a credit score, the so-called Sesame Index, is a universal feature of the workplace, where you get rewarded for public evidence of your capacity to think and speak in the right way. People really are speaking, if not singing, from the same hymn sheet and the long-held ambition of achieving total organisational alignment around values and goals has at last be achieved. You are in an age of 'conversational alignment'. Or are you?

Meanwhile, you and your colleagues, friends and family are busy creating fake identities where you can pursue other aspects of your personality more openly – a dark web outside the approved world of communication where you speak up more freely.

3. The rise of the 'bot' boss – an end to mood swings and bad days

Bosses have always been prone to having good days and bad days. The disciplines and practice of what makes for good conversational and dialogic exchange have been known about for years, but stress, egos and unconscious habits of mind keep leading bosses astray. How much better it is to live in an age when you know exactly what the boss wants because it's been programmed into them, and they also know how to respond perfectly well to you because it's been programmed into them.

Performance reviews and recruitment decisions are now made with considerably less discriminatory bias, allowing more diversity of voice in the workplace (although bias, inherent in the data sets the algorithms draw from, remains).

Conversational exchanges can no longer be governed by personality clashes and a lack of emotional regulation. Instead, they are governed by explicit rules. Your emotional state, values, motivations and capabilities are all considered and your bot boss relates to you in a way that is most effective at that point in time. Your boss no longer has to attend leadership development programmes which attempt, and fail, to alter behaviours. Your bot boss is simply programmed to be a good coach, mentor and advisor and to give you feedback in a way that you are most likely to be able to hear.

There is, of course, a lack of physicality and relational human connection. And you know that what you say to the bot is churned through an algorithm and fed into your appraisal, which means your sense of power difference and caution towards your boss bot remains persistent (and perhaps even increases). The rules of reason, truth and predictability are, however, constant and (apart from the odd glitch), based upon the most rational and organisational-centric algorithms.

4. Just the facts ma'am – how objective truth took control

Real time citation has removed the need to remember facts and data. Siri and Alexa and your prolific bots are the source of objective truth. They base their truth on the prevailing hierarchy of truth, which puts verifiable scientific knowledge at the top and is again wholly dependent on the human decision-making and ideology that has developed the algorithms and the data sets they draw from.

You have made your choice between two main schools that have emerged in relation to how to navigate truth. If you chose the first, you speak up and listen up in relation to what to do *in response to the truth,* rather than spending inordinate amounts of time debating and questioning *what the truth is* in the first place. You favour objective truth over subjectivity. If you like rule-based cultures, this fits well with you. Statements of do's and dont's have been programmed into algorithms and the truth equivalent of the Food and Drug Association (FDA) rules on the validity of facts and data. All you have to do is turn to them to tell you what the truth is likely to be.

If you chose the second school, you have trained yourself in the disciplines of critical thinking, the capacity to notice and critique assumptions (including the assumptions that underpin the algorithms that trawl through data to present the truth). You have learnt from key moments where society has suffered at the hands of fake news and propaganda-led feeds. You have realised the subjectivity at the heart of what had been prized as objectivity. You are pleased to see your organisation searching for people skilled at engaging with the nature of what makes something true or not. Your conversations focus on discerning multiple perspectives and *how you and others create shared meaning* from data through identifying assumptions and bias.

5. Bubble time – how truth became whatever our tribes want it to be

Donald Trump is seen as the trailblazer here. Truth does not exist outside what we already believe. The assertion of power makes truth its servant. This is George Orwell's *1984*,[5] where, if the powerful say so, 2 and 2 make 5.

We are fed information in our news feeds which focuses and amplifies the news (and vitriol) from our tribe and perspectives from others are squeezed out of earshot. The same occurs in our organisations. Powerful others (including those who have the capacity to understand algorithms and data) manipulate what employees get to hear. Points of view which chime with stated corporate values are projected on to our screens. Data and opinion which counter it are relegated along with opportunities for understanding and challenging our own perception of the world. 'Deepfakes', false footage and photos, which are so realistic they undermine truth and confuse, proliferate in order to swing opinion in the direction of the powerful.

The consequences of this depends in part on our capacity to realise what is happening and to care. It depends on whether this management of information is seen to improve our wellbeing as a society and our profitability as an organisation, or whether it is seen to strip away our freedom to speak and hear diverse views, leading eventually to dwindling agility, immorality and emaciated innovation in our organisations.

6. How much truth can you bear?

With the explosion of data that you now find at your disposal, you have had to make choices about where to focus your limited attention. Data is limitless, even though you are aware that your human capacity for assimilating it remains constrained.

You notice that some of your colleagues rarely seem to make eye contact anymore. They are mesmerised by, very possibly addicted to, their devices and the data appearing in front of their eyes. They prefer this data over and above their own experience and their embodied, visceral and intuitive knowing. Relationships with these colleagues have therefore become more and more transactional.

Others, however, are more mindful about how and when they use data, as well as when to trust it and when to question it. These colleagues seem to be using data to attempt to improve the way they are interacting with others. You notice they are driven by a strong belief in human connection and value relational quality first and foremost, although the balance between focusing on the device versus the human being is a hard one to strike.

Yet others have decided to step out of the technological fan club altogether and only use smart devices when absolutely essential.

Which choice do you think you'd make?

NAVIGATING THE FUTURE TRUTH

We don't know which of these scenarios will play out and to what extent. And there are of course, many, many others. It is probably fair to say though that we will have at our fingertips more data on ourselves and others than ever before. Notice that we say 'data' not 'truths' because behind the data we are presented with will be an algorithm. This trawls through data sets that mirror societal discrimination and emphasises some information while downplaying other information.

Given this, there are a number of important questions to ask ourselves in relation to how we will navigate speaking up and listening up through the TRUTH framework.

THE FUTURE OF SPEAKING TRUTH

Here are some thoughts and key questions for you to consider relating to whether and how you and others in your organisation might speak up in the future.

Trusting your opinion

An explosion in data might give you more confidence in your opinions because you can seek evidence. Or it might confuse you as you struggle to sift through information and know whether it is reliable and valid. Trusting yourself to speak up will be affected by:

- how you'll judge the sources of your knowledge and whether data will rule or whether embodied knowing, experience and intuition will still count.

- whether access to more data will give you confidence in your views or whether the proliferation of fake data and deepfakes will mean that you become just more confused, knowing that any perspective can be refuted with yet more data.

Risk of speaking up

Recent developments such as the #MeToo movement show how personal risk can be socialised. No longer do you have to shoulder the burden for speaking up on your own as alliances can be pulled together on a just-in-time basis. But risks could be amplified and new ones created. The inadvisable comment made in an unguarded moment can now be weaponised against you. Whatever you put out into the public domain may well last for ever and can be used in contexts beyond your control. Perception of risk will depend on the following:

- If you'll be able to sift through your various communication channels, find allies and speak up with collective power.

- If your every word is recorded and collated by algorithms which determine how you are seen by others, you'll face even greater risks in speaking up against the majority or politically acceptable story.

- If the increased data at your fingertips will aide you to speak up *skilfully* and therefore lead you to perceive less risk.

Understanding politics

How people use and manage data is never neutral – it serves a purpose. For example, in 2013, in an attempt to experiment with influencing users' emotions and moods, Facebook manipulated the newsfeeds of 689,003 users without their knowledge (or consent).[6] Data and its use is a battlefield being fought by people who are pursuing their own agenda – and in most cases they are very attached to the importance and validity of their purpose. So long as this 'wild west' phase of the emerging data economy is in play, it places an ever-increasing responsibility on individuals to realise that what they are told and what they choose to share is truly problematic. Politics will influence whether:

- technology will give you more or less sight of other people's interests and agendas in the future.

- you will have more advice via personal bots as to how to motivate and influence others – and whether that advice is effective.

- the games we all play simply heighten the political minefield around speaking up. For example, might gaming the algorithms mean that, if you are politically savvy, you speak up only in certain contexts, with certain people, in certain ways?

Titles

The technology of the future might at last make recruitment and evaluation at work less biased on the titles of age, gender and race. However, algorithms can simply reinforce the taken-for-granted habits of the existing social order – 'old titles in, old titles out' to rephrase the well-known computing insight of 'garbage in, garbage out'.

Our labels are group- and context-dependent so our speaking up will be influenced by how we as a society alter our perceptions of labels and add new ones. For example, titles associated with being a technologist may carry more and more weight. But, who knows, maybe in the future it will be those who wear the label of philosopher or sociologist that may be conferred higher status. As data about our personal state becomes more visible to others, maybe the most important labels will be around how the algorithm judges our mood in the moment, and whether or not we are in a fit state to be bought into a conversation, stay in it, or make a decision. Titles will be affected depending on:

- whether technology will help you to find your voice by reducing title bias in processes such as promotion rounds and recruitment.
- whether discrimination persists via the partial data sets that the algorithms draw upon, the ethical choices relating to the code and persistent social habits.
- who will get left out and forgotten in the future. If you have limited access to technology, will you be silenced?

How-to

Speaking up in the new digital world will require an ease with engaging with others across a wide range of different technologically enabled platforms. Although we will be equipped with more advice and data about how to speak up well, it will take real discipline not to be distracted by visual and other messages coming in from a myriad of sources. New and old technologies, such as emails, can strip out contextual data and so we will need to remain vigilant about how to speak up in a way that can be heard. Whether you are more or less able to know how to speak up will depend on:

- your personal bot's ability to advise you skilfully on what to say, to whom, where and when.
- the degree to which you still prioritise personal contact and your intuition.
- your ability to be present and contributing in technologically enabled forums. Will you speak up with more impact, or will the flurry of multiple, competing voices make it much harder to be heard?

THE FUTURE TRUTH OF LISTENING UP

It is as difficult to ascertain the effects of technology on listening up to others in the future as it is to examine how our own voices will be amplified or diminished. Here are some thoughts to reflect upon.

Trust in others' opinions

As the lack of trust in information sources continues, and very probably grows, the temptation to stay in your own information bubble and trust those who you've always trusted, may well reinforce a lack of belief in the opinion of others. However, there is the potential, as never before, to hear more points of view – and to be reminded to do so. At the heart of the matter remains whether we have a genuine belief in the value of the experience of others. You will need to decide:

- which sources of authority you'll trust, from government to business leaders to media channels to celebrities.

- whether to retreat into a world of self-curated truth bubbles which reinforce what you already know, or want to know, to be true. Or whether you will question and purposefully ensure you hear alternative views.

- who to listen to, in particular whether you'll end up limiting your attention to those who are equally savvy in the use of technology. How will you hear from those alienated or squeezed out from accessing tech through a lack of resources?

Risk

Technology can and will increasingly connect tops, middles and bottoms of organisations as never before. People can be seen and exposed as never before. This was seen, for example, in the global walkout at Google in response to a *New York Times*[7] article revealing the organisation had protected senior executives accused of sexual misconduct.

With technology's capacity for facilitating great connection comes great responsibility. It may not reduce power distance but could bring hierarchical power into people's faces in a much more immediate and potentially frightening way. For example, one of our interviewees spoke of his shock when he received a personal email from the CEO (who he'd never met) at 2am disagreeing with a decision he had made.

The need to understand that others may find you intimidating and to mitigate that fear remains paramount if you want them to speak up to you. You'll need to determine the following:

- the ways in which technology can enable you, with its analysis tools, to see when others find you scary. You'll decide whether to listen to suggestions from your devices on how to reduce the fear of others through saying and doing different things.

- how you can use multiple forums on different platforms to enable you to find ways of communicating with different people in a way that they feel is safe.

Understanding politics

As more and more goes on the record, is recorded, filmed and kept as a permanent audit trail of documented contribution, so politics gets more complicated. What gets expressed in public forums may become more superficial as people become more cautious. If you are regarded as powerful, the onus may increasingly fall on you to make your political agenda explicit, because in the face of uncertainty, others will play it safe and you will never hear their truth. Negotiating politics will require you to:

- decide how to use technology and the data presented to you, to gauge other people's motivations and their 'truth-telling' reputation
- skilfully use the tools and channels at your disposal to get to the real story – the one behind the smoke screen of what others want you to hear.
- navigate any confusion about what to believe if gaming the algorithm simply ends up increasing the political minefield.

Titles

Working at their best, well-designed data programmes may be able to strip away our unconscious biases and enable us to hear without recourse to our traditional need to socially categorise and pigeonhole. It might be that we will step into an age of listening without title. Although given human beings' capacity to create distinctions and status hierarchies we suspect that new categories will emerge and the old ones will find ways of being sustained. If you have the title of leader and expertise becomes more democratic, 'leader' may acquire a more facilitative meaning. If this is the case, listening may be imperative. The way we evolve titles in the future and determine which ones count will affect who you listen to. This raises the questions:

- Will the technology at your fingertips allow you and remind you to listen without discrimination – or at least with less bias?
- What titles will be applied to you that make you more or less scary to others in the future?

How-to

We may well reap the benefit of real-time data telling us how well we are actually listening and how listened to the person we're with is feeling. The technology that tracks our quality of listening could be as ubiquitous as a Fitbit is now. We will have to hold the tension between being fed automated suggestions and recommendations about what questions to ask, knowing when to put our apps down and trust our intuitive knowing and figuring out when to hold silence. Your capacity to know how to listen will depend on whether:

- you will use technology to connect more deeply to others than ever before and to listen to alternative perspectives.
- you will decide that your capacity for mindful attention and authentic presence is of utmost importance.
- AR will enable you to be present 'in person' with a more diverse group of people.

OUR ETHICAL AWARENESS, VIEWS AND CHOICES SHAPE OUR FUTURE

It is all but impossible to write about our future as a society without being an unknowing advocate for what our own culture sees as right and proper, in terms of its social and intellectual priorities. In thinking about the possibilities of the future for our artificial, augmented and algorithmic world we ran hard up against our western, individualistic views about the good society.

We nodded along in agreement when we listened to those we interviewed espouse the need for clear governance of the tech sector which guarded the rights of individuals. Then we realised our bias as we spoke to others soaked in the modern Chinese tradition and the priority that culture gives to the power of the political party. A belief in the primary importance of individuals and their rights for TRUTH is something that the children of the western enlightenment tradition take as axiomatic – not so for that great technological force, the Chinese Communist Party.

Perhaps the starting challenge for all of us is to notice what we take as obvious, and how that shapes how we view and make ethical choices about the future.

As for the technology firms themselves, they find themselves at a critical moment in time. Will we as society construct them to be broadly good for people, offering freedom and improved productivity, or as forces which increase the distance between the haves and the have-nots, that oppress, manipulate and silence? Facebook is living with the shadow of its founder's abrasive and strictly commercial view of the world as recorded in the 2004 instant messenger log of Mark Zuckerberg: 'Yeah so if you ever need info about anyone at Harvard. . . Just ask. . . I have over 4,000 emails, pictures, addresses. . . People just submitted it. . . They 'trust me'. . . Dumb Fucks.'[8]

Our future use of technology is being shaped by assumptions about people, relationships, politics and economics which are going to run into some flat contradictions with each other – and with people's view about what is socially acceptable. Speaking up and listening up has perhaps never been more important as we make profoundly consequential ethical choices which shape whose voice will get heard and whose voice will be silenced in the future.

Will we have the capacity to be patient, thoughtful and ethical in the choices we make now? Or will we be swept along in an unstoppable, breathless tide of technological applications, unable to pause for thought?

The choices we make *now* as our future evolves are shaped according to who speaks up and who listens. Thus, our existing power structure informs the power structure of tomorrow.

If you are in a position of power, the weight of that responsibility needs to be fully and humbly acknowledged.

KEY MESSAGES

- Technology is not value neutral – it will get used in a way that fits with the existing patterns of power and advantage.

- The future could be a heaven and/or hell depending on who and where you are in the system – and we'll only really know when we get there.

- Without trust we will retreat into islands of self-curated truth. Safety remains paramount. We will speak only if we believe our words, forever recorded, will not be used against us and we will listen only if we deeply hold a desire to be challenged by different perspectives.

- The opportunity to connect and create for the collective good will be extraordinary. The ethical choices we have to make to achieve that though make speaking and listening up more profoundly important than ever.

If you do only one thing now, ask the question 'What do we know *won't* change?' the next time someone says technology is changing everything.

NOTES

1. Groth, Iaf and Nitzberg, Mark (2018) *Solomon's Code: Humanity in a world of Thinking Machines.* Pegasus Books.
2. Rowling, J.K. (1998) *Harry Potter and the Chamber of Secrets.* Bloomsbury Publishing.
3. https://hbr.org/2017/11/a-managers-guide-to-augmented-reality
4. https://hbr.org/2018/03/how-to-think-for-yourself-when-algorithms-control-what-you-read
5. Orwell, George (2004) *1984.* Penguin Classics New Ed.
6. Fry, Hannah (2018) *Hello World: How to be Human in the Age of the Machine.* WW Norton & Company, p.42.
7. Kantor, Jodi and Streitfeld, David (2015) Inside Amazon: wrestling big ideas in a bruising workplace' *New York Times,* 15 August.
8. Fry, Hannah, p.25.

CHAPTER 8

SIX COMPASS POINTS ON THE WAY TO TRUTH

E very moment we are with others, in person or virtually, we make choices about what to say and what not to. Whether to say it like it is, deliver a politically motivated point, enthusiastically speak up with an idea, or remain silent. We make choices about when to listen and when not to. Whether to empathise, intently learn, ignore, daydream, judge or prepare our next statement.

Over time, these choices form patterns and create habits.

Collectively, our individual habits coagulate and form cultural norms, political games, safe processes and dangerous ones, opportunities for creative insight and for straight-jacketed conformity in our workplaces, our communities and homes.

These cultures then dictate how we must and do behave. With time and persistence, they put down roots and stick. Eventually they might even prescribe how our children will act. We tend to comply with the rules because we are social animals who need to belong, to be accepted and liked – and also because we believe they must have worked well enough for us to have got this far in life. So in a team of engaged, compassionate and respectful colleagues we speak up despite ourselves and our confidence and skill build and build. When the rules are 'It's safe to speak up' and 'You are expected to speak up', then we comply and become part of a generative culture.

In a politically motivated, distrusting group full of intrigue and clandestine conversations, we stay silent about anything that might be seen as contentious. It seems too risky to upset the status quo, and anyway, we don't have a moment in our busy lives to consider how we might begin to do something different. Speaking up becomes seen as onerous and unsafe, and a degenerative culture of silence and inauthenticity takes hold, where only the words which fit into the learnt rules get spoken.

If we feel uneasy in such a culture, then we blame others. We accuse them of lacking the courage to speak up, or talk nebulously about the negative culture of the group. And all the time, deep down we are disappointed with ourselves for not quite having the impact in our lives that we know we are capable of having, if only we could step outside of the rules that have us all in their grip.

Speaking and listening up *matters* deeply to each and every one of us. In big obvious ways when someone dramatically exposes wrongdoing or brings an impossibly important idea to the table. But also in day-to-day, mundane ways which do nothing short of shaping, imperceptibly, over time, the cultural norms of societies.

In this book we ask you to pause a moment to consider and pay attention to those specific moments and situations when you speak up and when you stay silent, when you listen and when you don't. We want you to notice what these habits give and cost you, when they serve you and others well, and when they sell you and others short.

We seek to deepen your awareness of why you make the decisions that you do and invite you to examine the consequences of your actions, or inactions. To speak up and to be heard is an act of existential validation – proof that we matter in the world, which is why being silenced and being ignored hurts so much and does so much damage. This is a call to reflect on something that shapes and gives meaning to your life and the lives of those around you. It is not confined to the workplace.

Here we will summarise our key messages, generated from our research findings. These are offered as a kind of compass so that you can set your direction towards skilfully knowing and navigating your TRUTH and helping others do the same.

This compass is offered to those of you who wish for (even) more transparency, authenticity, respect and compassion in those relationships which define who you are and the quality of your life.

COMPASS POINT #1: SPEAKING UP IS RELATIONAL

Our choice of whether or not to speak up is made in relation to our context, history and prior experience. It is dependent upon those that we are speaking up to in the here and now. Yet the call for others to 'speak truth to power' so often emerges as an individualistic, accusatory challenge to the least powerful. 'They should speak up more!', 'They should have the courage of their convictions!' and 'If they want change then they just need to speak up and make it happen!' It is presented as an act that is independent of social pressures and severable from the prevailing pattern of power, authority and group rules.

We know, however, that we will not speak up unless there is a chance someone will listen and unless we value what we have to say enough to bear the consequences. The responsibility therefore lies not just with the speaker but with the listener and everyone who is part of the wider group that governs the rules as to who has the right to say what to who.

If we want relationships which are more open and authentic, then we must work at speaking up *and* listening up in the specific context of our social setting. Focusing only on the speaker is like trying to choreograph a world-class, romantic, breath-taking waltz – with only one person and with no attention to the musicians or the tune they're playing. The speaker and listener come hand in hand – inseparable and in constant relationship, nested in society's rules. We must work with all of this in order to effect change.

COMPASS POINT #2: WE THINK WE ARE BETTER THAN OTHER PEOPLE (AND WE ARE PROBABLY WRONG)

Time and again we abdicate our own responsibility to improve the way we speak and listen up because we are more focused on how bad others are at it. We assume we are essentially approachable and would be brilliantly open with our views, if only others would just let us be. If *they* would just change, we would be even better.

In our survey results we see clearly that nearly every respondent thinks they are better than their boss. Yet, ask that respondent's direct reports and you get a different perspective. Because we don't speak up to one another openly, we remain in blissful ignorance of how we are experienced by others. We see ourselves as being outside, being other than, the culture we play an active part in creating.

Indeed, even if we are surrounded by some of the most appalling political, inauthentic and self-obsessed people, there is always a possibility of improving *our own* signals that we send into the system. Our determined capacity to learn and improve and inspire others with how we skilfully navigate and disrupt cultural norms of silence affects change far more than sitting back, tut-tutting and waiting impatiently for our colleagues, especially our bosses, to get better at this.

In every meeting and conversation we're part of, that we find unsatisfactory or scintillating, we need to ask ourselves: 'What's my part in creating this experience?'

COMPASS POINT #3: HOW WE SEE POWER MEDIATES EVERYTHING

Our perception of our relative power dramatically affects whether and how we speak up and listen up. Yet we rarely notice, yet alone question, the often simplistic and static notions which lie behind our initial assumptions of power difference. Our tendency is to simply let our minds form a view which then directs our actions. Or, if we cannot get clarity on our relative status and authority, we play it safe and do nothing.

We often portray and think about power as if it were a thing, a possession, an objective something which is limited in supply. We think of some as having power and others as not. The CEO has power and the middle manager doesn't. The white, male, privately educated boss has power and the person from a minority doesn't.

When we relate to another person, we inevitably seek to determine our relative power. This helps us to know how to act. Our view, however, is subjective and it changes according to context, mood and the current preoccupations of society's views on who should speak, who shouldn't and whose voice counts.

It is more illuminating and liberating if we see power in three ways: subjective, dynamic and contextual. This allows us to see that our sense of authority changes according to circumstances, that our view of being powerless is not an objective fact, and while we assume others may see themselves as powerful, that might not represent their internal experience.

The questions we ask ourselves then become 'When and why do I feel powerful and powerless?' and 'What are the assumptions behind this and how might they be challenged?' And the questions we ask together become 'How are we constructing power here?' and 'What do we assume conveys authority and status and what are the consequences of seeing power this way?'

Then we bring power out of the shadows. Then we can start to alter habits and culture.

COMPASS POINT #4: WE ARE BLIND TO OUR OWN POWER AND THEREFORE TO HOW WE SILENCE OTHERS

Although we tend to notice when we feel powerless, we are less likely to consciously realise that we are considered powerful by others and even less likely to acknowledge that others may be intimidated by us.

We tend to think of ourselves as approachable. We can't imagine why others would falter and if we see them doing this, blame is placed at their feet. 'Honestly, it's not as if I'm scary – they just need to speak up for goodness sake!'

We are slightly more likely to acknowledge our power if we occupy a high-ranking label such as CEO, although even then we can forget the implications of it. When we are 'just a normal manager', or indeed when we lack a formal hierarchical title, we can forget that others could still find us intimidating because of our gender, race, age, personality, appearance, network, or simply because we happen to remind them of someone that is or was powerful at some stage of their life.

It is imperative to acknowledge our own power and reflect on the situations where others might see us as powerful and stay silent, or speak up to us with a polished version of the truth or a political line that they want us to pass on. Yet this is often our biggest blind spot, which is kept in place by taken-for-granted phrases such as 'We're all equal here' or, for more senior people, 'I'm still the same person I've always been.'

COMPASS POINT #5: TRUTH DEFINES OUR ACTIONS AND OUR IMPACT

Our choices to speak and listen are informed by many things and we may be more or less aware of these in the moment. Our research has shown five issues to be particularly relevant and therefore five areas which we can reflect and work on to improve our conversations. The TRUTH framework describes these:

- How much do you **T**rust the value of your opinion. . . and that of others?

- What are the **R**isks you face in speaking up. . . and others face in speaking up to you?

- Do you **U**nderstand the politics of what does and doesn't get said to who?

- Are you aware of the **T**itles and social labels you put on others and others put on you and how they shape what gets said and is left unsaid?

- Do you know **H**ow to choose the right words and the right time to speak up and invite people to speak up to you?

Rigorous inquiry in each of these areas has to start with seeking to notice what our current TRUTH habits are. Then we have to work with those habits rather than wish them away or ignore them. Through doing this we begin to know the amazing complexity of our moment-by-moment interactions and we open up possibilities for different choices and habits.

COMPASS POINT #6: OUR CHOICES DEFINE OUR LIVES – AND THE LIVES OF OTHERS

Do you feel proud of the way you have behaved and acted in the world today? Did you admire the actions of those you worked with today?

While considering your response to these questions it is difficult to see how you wouldn't include in your reflections what you and those you work with chose to say and how you and they listened. If you remain a bystander when a colleague is treated unfairly, if you stay silent when your peer challenges your boss, despite you having the same grievances, if you're irritated by that persistent idea you have which could improve a product, service or relationship but you keep quiet through lack of confidence, or if you fail to share your successes when asked by your boss's boss, then little by little your sense of self-worth is undermined. Little by little others become disappointed in you.

If, however, you are seen to clearly speak when your values are under threat, when others are treated badly, if you offer ideas and shrug it off when they don't land and keep experimenting until they do, then you feel alive and liberated and others look to you as a role model.

If you speak over others, play the tick-box game of asking others their opinions while not really caring what they say, if you are too busy to engage and connect with those you work with, then again, in time, you will feel uneasy and others around you will gradually give up. You will have created a culture of silencing others and cut yourself off from anything but your own echo chamber.

Whereas if you move towards others with curiosity, if you treat them with respect and see them grow as you deeply listen to them, if you show them how you have been affected by what you heard, then you may feel satisfied and others may feel gratitude, warmth and respect. You will have created a culture of mutual exchange where people seek to hear and be heard, be moved by what they say and what others say to them. This is a world of learning rather than biased confirmation.

Your habits affect whether you feel proud of yourself or disappointed and whether others see you as a role model or as an obstacle to be overcome or worked around.

SETTING THE COMPASS TODAY

What conversation could you have differently today? If you were to change just something small about what you say or how you say it, who you listen to and how deeply, what would it be? If you could change someone else's life for the better, just a little bit, by saying or listening to something differently, what would it be?

We're not asking you to be perfect, or somebody you're not. We seek an expansion – one conversation at a time – in your capacity to live fully, learn, love, create and inspire.

It is our sincere hope that this book contributes to this.

APPENDIX: OUR RESEARCH

The purpose of our research is to make a positive difference to how people speak up and are heard at work. The methods we choose aim at engaging with the world of work as it is, deeply, rigorously and pragmatically, from multiple perspectives.

We approached the research that this book is based on with the following assumptions:

- Truth and power in the workplace are not objective and cannot be reduced to single, all-encompassing definitions. They are, to us, 'social constructs'[1] that exist within a specific context, a specific network of relationships and the unique qualities of a specific workplace. They are intimately bound up with each other.

- A workplace researcher is not the same as someone working in a laboratory. They are active participants in creating a particular point of view (story) about how truth and power are spoken of. In this case, inevitably, our own relationships to power, and how we experience who we see as powerful others, shaped the truth that we reported and noticed.[2]

- Different labels, for example, 'researcher', 'coach', 'tutor' and 'consultant', result in people engaging with us in very different ways. This has to be rigorously reflected upon and active choices need to be made in the research process as a result.

- As we research with others, we may alter the way those involved understand their world. Our *methods* (as well as our final publications and outputs) are therefore likely to lead to changes in the way our interviewees, survey respondents, workshop attendees and co-operative inquiry group members relate with their colleagues in dialogue. This might then, in turn, alter the organisational systems they are part of. Seen like this, our research process becomes an intervention in its own right and has required robust consideration of the corresponding ethical issues.[3]

- Research happens in the midst of life and not as a discrete project. There is no meaningful separation between the different professional and personal roles we play and so all conversations and experiences become part of the 'research' work.[4]

Given this messy, multi-perspectived and subjective view of how truth and power operate in the workplace we engaged with a multi-method approach consisting of the following:

- **One-to-one interviews:** We interviewed over 150 people between 2015 and 2018. Some were on the record, while the vast majority were off the record (we noted the ironies in asking others to 'speak up' to us about speaking up). They are offered in this book with a varying degree of depth of disguise and anonymity. Most were written up, reviewed and formally approved, while some were not as people either did not respond to requests to review the notes (in which case the stories were not used), or simply agreed to leave it to our discretion to use the output wisely.

- **Two major surveys:** The first one, that we called a 'diagnostic', emerged to support the initial inquiry phase and gave us over 500 individual responses. In 2018 a quantitative and qualitative 'Speaking Truth to Power' survey was designed and distributed globally. To date, it has received over 3,500 responses. A report entitled 'Speaking Truth to Power', which focuses specifically on this latter survey, can be downloaded at www.meganreitz.com[5] along with details of the diagnostic and original research report (entitled 'Being Silenced and Silencing Others').

- **Ethnographic studies:** Our research and other professional work since 2015 has seen us engaging with staff at all levels through sustained periods of organisational life. We have been immersed in 12 different organisations – sometimes formally contracting to research, other times taking a lead to develop specific initiatives to facilitate 'truth speaking to power'. Ethnography entails participating in formal and informal workplace activities, observation and interviews.[6]

- **Co-operative inquiries:** Co-operative inquiry[7] (CI) brings a group together at regular intervals to discuss a topic of mutual interest, devise actions and then reflect upon the results of those actions. All members of the group have roles as both researchers and research-subjects and as authors we fully participated. Our first CI group met from 2015 to 2016 and the second from 2017 to 2019. In all, 18 people participated with a wide range of organisational functions (most were senior level). The groups explored their personal experience of speaking up and being spoken up to in their workplaces *and* in the CI group itself. This focus on real-time reflection on power and voice enables CI to uncover and analyse in-the-moment thoughts, feelings and responses associated with speaking and listening.

- **Research and application workshops:** Since 2015 we have individually and jointly run approximately 100 workshops, initially to explore the emerging insights and frameworks, and latterly to test the usefulness of these insights for people going about their day-to-day working life.

- **A comprehensive review of management literature:** Closely supported by Viktor Nilsson at Ashridge, we reviewed over 50 papers linked to our field. Our literature review also built on Megan's doctoral thesis[8] and her role as a professor and supervisor on Ashridge's Executive Doctorate in Organisational Change.[9] John's contribution drew on his near twenty-year association with both the Ashridge Doctorate and Masters in Organisational Change, which has seen him write with and research the theory and practice of both the students and faculty of these programmes.[10]

- **Social and professional conversations:** Our personal and professional lives as coaches, advisors and tutors brings us into contact with hundreds of people from all walks of life – and with perspectives on work that are rarely admitted to in public.

- **First-person research, personal supervision and reflection:** Over the life of this research, we've been supervised by colleagues and also taken to time to reflect on how we experience truth and power being constructed between us. We have engaged in 'first person' action research,[11] which involves dedicated attention and reflection on our own habits of conversation. Megan has used her mindfulness practice in support of this, while John has continued his long-standing work with his Jungian analyst to notice his own patterns in action.

As a result of this process, we are able to claim that we have created insights which are focused on being useful to people as they go about their lives in complex, emergent workplaces, unique to them.

NOTES

1. See Gergen, K. (2009) *An Invitation to Social Constructionism.* Sage, UK.
2. Coghlan, David (2011) Action research: exploring perspectives on a philosophy of practical knowing. *The Academy of Management Annals* 5 (1), 53–87.

3. King, K. (2010) World views matter. In King, K. and Higgins, J. (Eds) *The Change Doctors: Re-Imagining Organisational Practice.* Farringdon: Libri publishing, pp. 2–4.

4. Coleman, G. (2015) Core issues in modern epistemology for action researchers: Dancing between knower and known. In Bradbury, H. (Ed.) *Handbook of Action Research.* London: Sage, 3rd ed., pp. 392–400.

5. www.meganreitz.com

6. Denzin, N. K. (1997) *Interpretive Ethnography.* Thousand Oaks, CA: Sage.

7. Heron, J. and Reason, P. (2001) The practice of co-operative inquiry: Research 'with' rather than 'on' people. In Reason, P. and Bradbury, H. (Eds) *Handbook of Action Research: Participative Inquiry and Practice.* London: Sage, pp. 179–188.

8. Reitz, M. (2015) *Dialogue in Organizations: Developing Relational Leadership.* Palgrave McMillan, UK.

9. http://www.hult.edu/en/executive-education/qualifications/doctorate-in-organizational-change/

10. King, K. and Higgins, J. (2014) *The Change Doctors: Re-imagining Organisational Practice.* Farringdon: Libri.

11. Marshall, J. (2016) *First Person Action Research.* Sage, UK.

INDEX